Making the Transition from an Intensive English Program to Mainstream University Courses
An Ethnographic Study

Front cover photograph courtesy of Robert A. Case, Jr.

MAKING THE TRANSITION FROM AN INTENSIVE ENGLISH PROGRAM TO MAINSTREAM UNIVERSITY COURSES
AN ETHNOGRAPHIC STUDY

Emerson D. Case

Mellen Studies in Education
Volume 96

The Edwin Mellen Press
Lewiston•Queenston•Lampeter

Library of Congress Cataloging-in-Publication Data

Case, Emerson D.
　Making the transition from an intensive English program to mainstream university courses : an ethnographic study / Emerson D. Case.
　　p. cm. -- (Mellen studies in education ; 96)
　Includes bibliographical references and index.
　ISBN-0-7734-6353-4
　　1. English language--Study and teaching--Foreign speakers. 2. English language--Study and teaching (Higher)--United States. 3. Mainstreaming in education--United States. 4. Language and education--United States. 5. Concentrated study. I. Title. II. Series.

PE1128.A2C365 2004　　　　　　　　　　　　　　　　　　　　2004049898
428'.0071 22

```
This is volume 96 in the continuing series
Mellen Studies in Education
Volume 96 ISBN  0-7734-6353-4
MSE Series ISBN  0-7734-935-0
```

A CIP catalog record for this book is available from the British Library.

Copyright © 2004 Emerson D. Case

All rights reserved. For information contact

The Edwin Mellen Press	The Edwin Mellen Press
Box 450	Box 67
Lewiston, New York	Queenston, Ontario
USA 14092-0450	CANADA L0S 1L0

The Edwin Mellen Press, Ltd.
Lampeter, Ceredigion, Wales
UNITED KINGDOM SA48 8LT

Printed in the United States of America

CONTENTS

Acknowledgments		i
Preface by Christopher M. Ely		iii
Chapter One:	An Overview of the Study	1
Chapter Two:	Articulation Studies	11
Chapter Three:	Methodology	31
Chapter Four:	Case Studies of Six Former IEP Students	49
	Samory	50
	Mari	70
	Romulo	91
	Fernanda	116
	Lyn	142
	Ayla	158
Chapter Five:	Discussion of the Findings	173
Chapter Six:	Summary of the Research, Suggestions for Intensive English Programs, and Recommendations for Further Research	209
Bibliography		227
Index		233

ACKNOWLEDGMENTS

This book comes out of my experiences over the past decade as a doctoral student and intensive English instructor. Thus, I am greatly indebted to those kind and generous teachers, colleagues, and friends without whose assistance over the years this project would not have been completed.

First, I owe a special debt of gratitude to Christopher M. Ely at Ball State University, who served not only as teacher and supervisor, but as mentor as well. His generosity and expertise helped to make my experiences as a graduate student and an IEP instructor both productive and enjoyable.

My greatest appreciation also to two great teachers and readers, Dr. Elizabeth Riddle and Dr. Herbert Stahlke, both of Ball State University, for their time, energy, and insight into earlier drafts of this work.

Thanks also to Dr. John C. Crawford , professor emeritus from the University of North Dakota, for getting me started in the field of linguistics and for his continued support.

I owe a great deal of thanks also to my good friend and co-conspirator, Stephen R. Lewis, who helped me in uncountable ways over the years.

My heartfelt thanks also to the six anonymous people documented in this book who generously offered up their time and experiences, making this study possible.

A special thank you to my parents, Robert and Lois Case, for all the support over the years.

And as always, I owe my greatest debt of gratitude to my wonderful wife, Meiqiong, for her patience, support, and faith.

PREFACE

Emerson D. Case's *Making the Transition from an Intensive English Program to Mainstream University Courses: An Ethnographic Study* is a groundbreaking work, both in the scope of its research and in its methodology. This book presents the first full-scale longitudinal investigation of the articulation of students from intensive English study to full academic work at a US university.

As important as Case's work is to our understanding of this transitional process, of equal value is the fact that he presents the field with, literally, an exemplary piece of scholarship. The study offers us a well-developed and sophisticated model for the type of qualitative research that can help advance our knowledge in many areas of second language acquisition and second language teaching.

The significance of this ethnography can perhaps best be appreciated by examining Case's work in the context of other research in this area. Previous studies on the transition of intensive English program students to academic programs, while exploring interesting aspects of the process, are characterized by various limitations. Some have focused only on the university writing or other language-oriented classes that IEP students take immediately after leaving the language program (e.g., Shuck, 1995). Other studies that have investigated the impact of IEPs upon later academic performance have employed one-time interviews or questionnaires, rather than utilizing a longitudinal research methodology (e.g., Christison & Krahnke, 1986).

Case's work provides the field with a much broader understanding of the articulation process, due in large part to the methodology he employs. The study is firmly grounded in the ethnographic tradition pioneered by, for example, Pelto and Pelto (1970) and Spradley (e.g., 1979) and continued by such scholars as Bernard (1995). Case's research reveals a solid understanding of the principles of such ethnography, no more clearly than in his extensive utilization of detailed notes taken at different levels of specificity, the depth and flexibility of his interviews, and his making of ever more extensive and intensive analyses based on his primary data.

One of the major strengths of this study is the degree to which it is situated within the context of the subjects' individual academic backgrounds. In addition, Case chose to work with the students in depth while they were still attending IEP classes, thus allowing him to sharply triangulate the interview data that they would provide after leaving the English program. Other methodological strengths of this research include the fact that Case selected students who represented a broad scope of cultural, academic, and personal backgrounds, enabling him to explore a diversity of personal variables. Of the six subjects, three were graduate students and three were undergraduates. The subjects represented South American, Asian, African, and Middle Eastern cultural backgrounds. The students also differed in their majors, amount of prior academic and work experience, and family situations.

Perhaps the most appealing aspect of Case's study is the wide-ranging nature of the research questions he raises, focusing on many issues in both the foreground and background of his subjects. In investigating factors that either facilitated or hindered the transition, he examines, for instance: knowledge, skills, and expectations the students brought with them from their prior experiences; features of the intensive program; actions the students took during their time at the university; and actions taken by academic class instructors.

Due to both the breadth of Case's research questions and the richness of his data, the conclusions that he is able to draw are often multi-layered and complex. One set of findings, for example, strongly suggests the importance of the students' prior linguistic, as well as content-based, experience in the articulation process. However, Case also shows how the impact of these background factors was mitigated or heightened by actions the students took when confronted with unexpected challenges in their academic courses. Some of the most interesting findings involve cultural mismatches between the students and their academic instructors and academic milieu. Subjects, for instance, from cultures which place a low emphasis on student-faculty interaction found it exceedingly difficult to approach course instructors, and also suffered from an inability to solicit personal assistance from their instructors. In addition, Case discovered major ramifications of mismatches between the students' learning styles and the teaching styles employed by their instructors.

Administrators and instructors in Intensive English Programs in the US will be greatly interested in Case's findings and recommendations regarding the role played by the IEP in preparing the students for their academic work, as well as his discussion of strategies which an IEP might employ to meet students' articulation needs in innovative ways.

In sum, Case's study clearly demonstrates the need for and benefits of extended ethnographic explorations in second language teaching and acquisition research. One hopes that other scholars will follow his example and carry out equally thorough and thoughtful longitudinal studies in our field.

Christopher M. Ely
Ball State University

BIBLIOGRAPHY

Bernard, H. R. (1995). Research methods in cultural anthropology. Newbury Park, CA: Sage Publications.

Christison, M. A., & Krahnke, K. J. (1986). Student perceptions of academic language study. TESOL Quarterly, 20, 61-79.

Pelto, P. P. & Pelto, G. H. (1970). Anthropological research: The structure of inquiry. New York: Harper and Row.

Shuck, G. (1995). Preparing for university writing courses: A survey of students' perceptions. Journal of Intensive English Studies, 9, 38-49.

Spradley, J. (1979). The ethnographic interview. New York: Holt, Rinehart and Winston.

CHAPTER ONE
AN OVERVIEW OF THE STUDY

Introduction

Each academic term, at colleges and universities across the United States, ever-increasing numbers of students descend upon the campuses that make up the American system of higher education. One segment of that population that has seen a particularly dramatic increase in the past fifty years is the population of international students, growing from 1.4% of the total students population in 1954-1955 to 4.6% of the total in 2002-2003. Despite wars, global recessions, political and financial crisis, and, natural disasters, the number of international students studying in U. S. colleges and universities has increased each year since 1954, with a record 586,323 international students attending American institutions of higher education in the school year 2002-2003 (Institute of International Education, 2003).

The impact that these students have on America and its educational system is far reaching. As *Open Doors 2002: Report on International Educational Exchange* points out, the impact of international students studying in the United States is not just felt on the campuses themselves, but across a wide spectrum of the American economy. "Student expenditures," it states, "include tuition and cost of living expenses for themselves, and often expenses associated with their spouse and dependents who accompany them to the United States." This impact is so large, they point out, that "The U. S. Department of Commerce ranked educational services as the nation's fifth largest service sector export in the year 2000, contributing $11 billion to the economy" (p. 5).

A further subdivision of this population of international students, a segment that the present study concerns itself with, has also seen a dramatic increase over the past several decades: international students enrolled in intensive English programs (IEPs). According to *Open Doors 2002*, IEP enrollments "were more affected by [the events of September 11, 2001] than those of degree programs because of the flexible and ongoing nature of Intensive English Programs" (p. 21). IEP enrollments have been affected by many different factors ranging from weak economic situations in many countries, concerns about student safety, and competition from other host countries (Institute for International Education, 2003) to frequent visa delays/denials and SARS [Severe Acute Respiratory Syndrome] (Young, 2003, p. 36). In spite of this, however, 51,179 international students were enrolled in IEPs in the calendar year 2002 (Institute of International Education, 2003). "Despite these difficulties," Dr. Allan E. Goodman, President and CEO of the IIE points out, "the United States remains the premier destination for foreign students" (Institute of International Education, 2003). As these numbers demonstrate, then, IEPs are undoubtedly providing a means of entry into institutions of higher for a considerable portion of international students studying in America.

These sizeable numbers, however, may be quite misleading. For many students, making the transition from an IEP to the mainstream university curriculum is not an entirely positive one. Smoke (1988) puts it very succinctly, writing, "ESL teachers remember the hopeful faces of students they helped guide through developmental ESL courses. When these teachers stop to ask former students how they are doing in content courses, too often the response is a shrug or a frown. These ESL students are struggling against enormous odds and in all too many cases are not succeeding in the American college system" (p. 11).

My decision to conduct this study grew out of just such reactions from my former students while I was an instructor in an intensive English program (IEP) at a medium-sized Midwestern American university. As Smoke states, "As their teachers, many of us ask ourselves what more can we offer these students to make their college experience more rewarding" (p. 11). While most would agree that this is a very important question in theory, in practice few studies have been carried out that help the teacher determine how this can be accomplished.

Previous research has been conducted that examines what factors predict mainstream academic success, such as certain background variables, language learning variables, or success on standardized tests. Some studies provide prescriptive descriptions of programs designed to assist in the transition to mainstream academic courses. Other investigations have been conducted that examine the intensive English program itself and its contribution to academic success. Still others have looked at what student perceive as their greatest needs. Only a small number of studies have examined the actual articulation process itself. No research has apparently been conducted that examines what happens to university level students as they are in the process of making the transition from an intensive English program to mainstream university courses.

This study seeks to determine what needs students have as they make this transition from an intensive English program to mainstream university courses and how an intensive English program can help to make such a transition more effective. It also seeks to provide a more accurate description of the articulation process than has previously been given. The focus of the present study is to provide data on what students go through from *their* perspective, in terms of *their* culture, rather than only from the perspective of such instruments as tests or formal assessments.

The present study provides a holistic examination of the process of transitioning from an intensive English program to mainstream university courses *as that transition occurs* over an extended period of time. It examines that process using a methodology, ethnography, that allows the discovery of what students know, or don't know, all from the perspective of the students themselves.

This study also seeks to provide intensive English program administrators and instructors with knowledge about, and a deeper understanding of, the processes their students go through as they enter into the mainstream university community. It also strives to advocate ways in which intensive English programs can prepare students for, and smooth over, this process. This understanding is necessary since many international students who are entering American universities are under-prepared linguistically and culturally to enter the community. In addition, this study can help students learn what they themselves can do to make the process easier and more productive.

The United States is undoubtedly the leader in providing the world with access to higher education. As Goodman points out, however, "At the national, state, and campus level, we need to take concerted action to insure that we retain that position" (Institute of International Education, 2003). I hope that the present study will serve as part of that concerted effort. As a starting point for understanding the process of articulation, this chapter will next look at the nature of intensive English programs and the students who populate them.

Intensive English Programs

According to Robert Kaplan (1997), "IEPs are many-splendored, many-faceted organisms" (p. 3). The genesis of the intensive English program is widely attributed to the English Language Institute at the University of Michigan in the years immediately following the Second World War (Barrett, 1982; Eskey, 1997). Because of this relatively short history, Eskey writes, "It is hardly surprising that IEPs cannot be described as "traditional" academic programs; IEPs are clearly new kids on the academic block" (p. 21).

Although IEPs are indeed "a many splendored thing," we can, according to Barrett (1982), identify certain characteristics which can be used to distinguish between what is an intensive English program and what is not. Barrett lists nine features in total. "First," he writes, "IEPs all have multilevel programs with respect to English proficiency," offering "ESL study on at least three levels: elementary, intermediate, and advanced." The second characteristic is that they all use a battery of standardized ESL subtests as an aid for initial placement and for measuring progress through the courses offered by the IEP (p. 1).

The third characteristic regards the type of courses offered by IEPs. "There is," Barrett states, "a recognition of the four major language skills: listening, speaking, reading, and writing," with a fifth area, grammar, also being recognized as playing a supplementary role to these four skills. The fourth criteria regards the IEP as being an entity which typically provides a service to a college or a university, and is therefore normally placed within the auspices of an academic department, a school or a college (p.2).

Fifth, according to Barrett, the typical IEP functions on a year-round basis which allowing IEP students to progress through the sequences of courses offered without being forced to experience lengthy gaps in between classes. The sixth characteristic deals with the amount of instruction received in the average IEP, which "offers from twenty to thirty hours of ESL instruction per week, for a total of 200 or more hours per session" (p.2).

The seventh criteria given by Barrett deals with the advising, as well as orientation, aspect of the IEP, many of which offer programs to help acquaint the student with the life they will experience on American campuses and help them understand what will be expected of them in their academic study. The eighth characteristic of an IEP deals with the nature of IEP students, who Barrett characterizes as "adults with high school diplomas, most of whom plan to pursue degree programs in American postsecondary institutions after reaching an adequate level of English proficiency" (p.2).

The final characteristic of an intensive English program deals with the administration of the IEP. "An IEP," Barrett writes, "is staffed with a director and core faculty who are professionally trained in teaching English as a second language (TESL) or linguistics" (p. 2).

In spite of having these characteristics, however, intensive English programs, Eskey points out, "cannot be described as 'traditional' academic programs" (p. 21). There are several reasons why they do not qualify as such. First, they serve non-traditional student populations. Second, they employ non-traditional faculty. Third, they feature non-traditional curricula directed toward non-traditional academic objectives. And finally, they are usually locked into non-traditional administrative and budgetary structures.

IEP students, Eskey points out, may eventually major in any of the traditional disciplines, but none will major in ESL, which means that IEP coursework is non-traditional, involving "many more instructional hours per week – often 25 to 30 – than the typical academic course load requires," which leads to a heavy teaching load for faculty. Additionally, the final objective of IEP work "is not the acquisition of a body of knowledge, as in most traditional fields of study, but the mastery of a particular set of language skills – the English skills required for success in U.S. university degree programs" (p. 24).

Thus, Eskey claims, ESL is regarded "as a means, not an end – a *pre*requisite to academic study – and therefore something very different from such traditional fields as literature or chemistry" (p. 24). In addition, IEP courses are nearly always *non*credit courses. And IEPs are almost never regarded as academic departments themselves, which leads to IEPs not achieving traditional academic status.

This leads to several problems, according to Eskey. One unfortunate result of this is that ESL students, "especially those enrolled in pre-admission IEPs, are often confused with native-speaking students who have failed to acquire the language skills required for university-level performance – that is, students in need of remedial course work" and that the IEP courses are "conducted at a lower intellectual level than traditional academic classes." All of this, "further marginalizes ESL instruction in a university context where accumulating credits toward a specific degree is the usual academic practice" (p. 24).

"IEP students are," Eskey states, "in short, a heterogeneous bunch with no obvious place in the academic pecking order and few natural advocates among university administrators, especially high-level administrators, or among faculty in more traditional fields" (p. 22).

Research Questions

In an attempt to better understand the processes that international students go through as they make the transition from an intensive English program to mainstream classes, ten primary research questions were developed. These questions are detailed and discussed below.

1. **What variables in the background of the informants were the most helpful in making the transition?**
2. **What variables in the background of the informants caused the most difficulties in making the transition?**

The first two questions in the study were asked in an attempt to help determine what variables informants themselves brought with them to the study. In this way, it was hoped that these variables could be separated from other variables, in an attempt to determine what variables intensive English programs could and could not control.

3. **Do undergraduate and graduate students go through similar or different processes as they make the transition?**

This question was asked to help determine what different needs undergraduate and graduate students have as they make the transition and to determine if those different needs should be addressed by intensive English programs and if students at different levels need to be prepared in different ways.

4. **What variables encountered in the environment were the most helpful in making the transition?**
5. **What variables encountered in the environment caused the most difficulties in making the transition?**

These two questions were asked to determine what variables found in the study could be considered out of the control of both the informants and the intensive English program. In this sense, an intensive English program would then know what issues to address and which issues are beyond their control.

6. What actions on the part of informants helped to make the transition smoother?

7. What actions on the part of informants caused the most difficulties in making the transition?

As the most important questions asked in the study, these two questions were asked to determine what variables informants themselves could control in an effort to determine what students in an intensive English program can do to help themselves (or hinder themselves) while making the transition, as well as to determine what actions can be taken by future intensive English program students that will help or hinder them.

8. What actions on the part of instructors helped to make the transition smoother?

9. What actions on the part of instructors caused the most difficulties in making the transition?

These two questions were also asked to determine what further variables on the part of instructors were out of the control of the informants, as well as in an effort to better inform instructors as to what they can do to make the transition easier and more productive for the international students who attend their classes.

10. What areas could the intensive English program improve on to make the transition smoother?

This question was asked to determine the perceptions on the part of informants of how the intensive English program could implement changes in an attempt to meet the perceived needs of the students who attend its classes, asking for specific and concrete examples of how those changes could be made.

Overview of the Study

Chapter One gives an overview of the study, providing a rationale for the study, a review of the relevant literature, and the research questions involved.

Chapter Two provides a complete review of the relevant literature on articulation studies at three different levels: 1) the elementary school level; 2) the secondary school level; and 3) the college/university level.

Chapter Three provides a detailed description of the methodology used in the study. It discusses the nature of ethnography, provides an overview of the informants and of the interviews, including the schedule of interviews and the specific questions addressed in each interview, gives an overview of the class observations conducted, discusses the data collection techniques used, and discusses the nature of the records kept.

Chapter Four provides detailed results of the case studies for each of the six informants in the study, including background information and specific descriptions of each of the interviews and class observations.

Chapter Five examines the data found in the study of each of the six informants, providing a point-by-point discussion of the research questions in relation to the data uncovered from each of the six informants and interprets their implications.

Chapter Six is a summary of the main findings of the study and presents its implications, as well as suggestions for further research and suggestions for future changes for intensive English programs.

A complete bibliography follows Chapter Six.

CHAPTER TWO
ARTICULATION STUDIES

Introduction

Harklau (1994) writes that the "demographic reality" of the number of bilingual education and ESL classes "has led educators to seek ways in which they might better articulate ESL and mainstream instruction and thus ensure a smooth transition." She continues, stating "Researchers have noted the paucity of closely detailed ethnographic descriptions comparing these two contexts which might serve as the basis for such approaches and facilitate the articulation and transition between ESL and the mainstream" (p. 242).

The following literature review seeks to provide an overview of the relatively small amount of research that has been conducted on the articulation process. The review will examine studies at three different levels: (1) the elementary school level; (2) the secondary school level; and (3) the college/university level.

The Elementary School Level

A very small number of the studies that have been carried out have been on the articulation process at the elementary school level. Shannon (1990) reports on a study conducted in two school districts in Connecticut in which two groups of English-Spanish bilingual program students were studied during their first year transitioning into an all-English program. The study examined two sets of transitioning students, a group of six third and fourth graders within one school and a group of seven students who had made the transition an elementary school into the sixth grade at a middle school. Shannon conducted participant observation in a number of different settings, with each site being visited for a full day once a week for six months, held informal interviews, examined various school records, and was even a guest in various students' homes. Shannon's study demonstrates, she claims, that "while language is a central concern and primarily the responsibility of the bilingual program, other issues are involved" (p. 341).

Shannon claims that her study demonstrated that the onus for the linguistic preparation for such transitioning students falls almost exclusively on the bilingual program itself. Once the students make the transition, however, the supports that the program offered these students are "stripped away." The assumption is, according to Shannon, that once the student has made the transition they are fully prepared to participate linguistically in mainstream classes. However, such students have not, in Shannon's words, "been transformed miraculously into an individual for whom English is their only language, one in which they have native-like fluency." Shannon believes that "the transitioned student internalizes her native language and culture after transitioning from bilingual programs while externally operating in the new, all-English environment." Because they are still dependent on their native language, Shannon writes, "It is no wonder, then, that the transition year is not of overwhelming success for most bilingual students who must build a new support system for coping and competing, and often must do this without assistance and guidance from teachers" (p. 341).

Shannon makes some specific suggestions. She writes, "Drawing upon and extending the students' experiences and knowledge could have enhanced the lesson and be made a part of a scaffold to support the students' learning." Further, "Not only would the bilingually schooled students benefit from a more relevant curriculum, all students would benefit from embedding context, making lessons less cognitively demanding and more socially interactive" (p. 333).

Shannon concludes by emphasizing that if educators "recognize the bilingual and bicultural assets that the students bring to the classroom, teaching and learning will be enhanced for all" (p. 342).

Another example of a study done at the elementary level can be found in the case study reported on in Willett (1995), which was part of a larger multi-year ethnographic study of graduate students and their families who were from various countries. As part of this larger study, the study reported on by Willett was concerned with four first-graders, three girls and one boy, acquiring English in a regular classroom.

For this study, writes Willett, "three girls categorized as limited English proficient students were audio-taped each morning as they participated in two regular classroom events - seatwork and recitation during language arts." Through the recordings, Willett was able "to capture the broader classroom discourse, the language of the interlocutors, and the sub-vocalizations of the ESL child wearing the recorder." Willett then transcribed the audiotapes which were subsequently checked for accuracy by a speaker of Arabic, Hebrew, and English. The author also took notes while the children were doing seatwork, as well as notes about the classroom's social and academic interactions, as well as the school and community's daily interactions. Artifacts from the classroom were also collected and the author was given access to school records, including test results, and subsequently conducted interviews with both the teacher and parents.

Although the author did not interview the children on any formal basis, she did experience daily interaction with them, and used casual conversation "to elicit their understanding about what was going on in the classroom." Certain transcripts were then selected on the basis of their theoretical interest, with at least one tape from each month being transcribed "in order to get a picture of the children's development over time."

Willett draws several conclusions. She writes:

> The girls strategically enacted and elaborated culturally shaped interaction routines to construct their social, linguistic, and academic competence (as locally defined). In the process of appropriating the ways of talking and thinking that constituted doing phonics seatwork, the girls also constructed desirable identities, social relations, and ideologies. Their ways and outcomes of working together, however, were governed by the micropolitics of the classroom. (p. 499)

Contrasting the girls' experiences with those of the only ESL boy in the classroom, she writes:

> The study shows how the micropolitics of gender and class worked to position the boy as a problematic learner and the girls as successful learners in this particular sociocultural setting. The findings of this study also illustrate that using the individual as the predominant unit of analysis in the study of language acquisition reveals only part of a very complex story. Moreover, the kinds of interactional routines and strategies used to construct relations, identities, and ideologies in this particular classroom were local, not universal. Those used in another cultural setting may have very different consequences. (p. 499)

The Secondary Level

Other studies on the articulation process have been carried out at the secondary level. One of the best studies conducted at this level is given in Harklau (1994), who describes a three and half year ethnographic study of second language learning experiences of immigrant students attending Gateview High School (a pseudonym) in the San Francisco Bay Area. The study "represented a unique opportunity to compare the same students' language learning experiences and behavior across ESL and mainstream contexts and to trace each student's high school career each year as they were making the transition from ESL classes into mainstream classes" (p. 242). This study determined that there were quite radical differences in both the goals and methods of organization of instruction when comparing Gateview's mainstream classrooms with ESL classrooms. The article also found large contrasts in how ESL classes and mainstream classes functioned in terms of how they helped socialize ESL students into American schools and society in general.

Based on the advice of the school's ESL teacher Carson (a pseudonym), Harklau selected four ethnic Chinese students as the sample group/case studies "because of their predominance in the ESL program." She then studied these students from four to seven semesters, through full school days and "in most cases on two consecutive days," in both their ESL classes and their mainstream classes, as they made the transition at Gateview. Harklau collected daily schoolwork and homework, and also had access to school records. In addition, Harklau reports, "Much of my contact with students occurred in informal conversation at lunch time, allowing students' emic perspectives on their experiences to unfold, while providing opportunities to guide the conversation, clarify, or raise a new subject when necessary. Between two and seven formal interviews up to one hour long were conducted with each student at less frequent intervals, when informal contact did not suffice" (p. 246).

In addition to the observations of the students themselves, their mainstream teachers were also briefly interviewed. "These teachers," Harklau states, "were asked to comment on each student's performance in their class and if they had had other experiences with ESL students in their classes." The study was eventually expanded, with supplemental interviews and observations of Taiwanese and Hong Kong immigrants being interviewed, with additional observations of Ethnic Chinese students in both mainstream English classes and Social Studies classes. "In total," writes Harklau, "315 hours of observations (165 hours in 56 mainstream classes, and 150 hours in ESL classes) and 38 formal interviews were conducted in addition to innumerable informal encounters that took place with students and school personnel during the three and half years of the study."

The study found, Harklau writes, that "the predominant activity in mainstream classrooms at Gateview was what Applebee (1981) has termed teacher-led discussion. Because the majority of students were native speakers of the language, the target language served an authentic communicative need, as the medium through which concepts needed to perform school tasks were communicated" (p. 251). Harklau found that, since they perceived themselves as talking to native speakers, the mainstream teachers observed in the study rarely adjusted their speech to accommodate the ESL students in their classes. Further, because they attempted to elicit answers by addressing questions to the entire class rather than individuals, "the students who could most loudly or confidently bid for the floor" were favored, which in turn allowed the ESL students to simply remain quiet. Harklau writes, "Some teachers noted that they wanted to spare nonnative speakers from being put on the spot. Because they were seldom required to participate in classroom interactions, second language learners were able to tune out many mainstream instructional activities entirely. They were not even paying particular attention to the input, much less engaging in interaction" (p. 251).

In contrast, in the ESL classes Harklau found that "Teacher-led discussion was also the predominant activity conducted through the spoken channel. However, qualitative differences existed in how discussion was organized and framed, differences which resulted in qualitatively superior input and richer, more frequent opportunities for interaction and spoken language output. Besides making input more comprehensible than in mainstream classrooms, Carson also created extended opportunities for students to interact and participate" (p. 252).

Harklau reports that "the content and course objectives of high school subject-area instruction presumed a relatively stable student population with a uniform knowledge base shaped by eight or nine years of previous instruction in

American elementary and middle schools." This contrasts sharply with Gateview's ESL program, in Harklau's view, which was constantly changing and adapting to student need. In addition, ESL students considered the ESL classes to be too easy. In spite of this, however, the ESL classes did give the students something that was lacking in mainstream classes: specific instruction in language that was designed to meet the linguistic needs of these students. Harklau reaches several main conclusions. She writes:

> The main advantage of mainstream classes was plentiful, authentic input that served a genuine communicative purpose - to transmit the content of school subject matter. The mainstream curriculum also provided students with rich and plentiful linguistic interaction through the written mode. However, the structure of mainstream instruction allowed few opportunities for extended interaction. Furthermore, L2 learners seldom received explicit feedback or instruction on the target language, leaving them to depend on somewhat faulty intuitions about language form. Finally, although the mainstream offered many social opportunities for language use and interaction with native speakers on the face of it, closer examination revealed that newcomers to U.S. society were seldom able to take advantage of such opportunities and perceived a barrier between themselves and U.S.-born peers. (pp. 266-267)

Harklau reports that ESL classes at Gateview, on the other hand, "provided students with language instruction and experiences not commonly available in the mainstream." This instruction focused on the productive use of both oral and written skills. Harklau writes, "Students were given explicit feedback on their linguistic production and were given appropriate instruction on linguistic principles and rules which could help them to monitor their own production. The ESL program also offered students readily available opportunities for counseling and peer social interaction." Nevertheless, the ESL courses were not without problems. "Students stigmatized ESL as easy and remedial," Harklau explains, "because instruction not only addressed their need for academic language that would facilitate transition to mainstream instruction, but also instructed them on the language used in everyday life and interaction." Harklau concludes, "The fact is that there was no truly appropriate education environment for L2 learners at Gateview. Rather, students' educational experiences were a makeshift response of a system fundamentally geared towards the instruction of native speakers of the language" (p. 267).

In a study done at the secondary level in Australia, Miller (2000) conducted an 18 month investigation that tracked immigrant students from an initial intensive English program to high school ESL courses to mainstream high school courses. Her focus was on "eliciting talk, listening to the students, and observing their interactions and their communications in several different settings" which included different schools, their ESL classrooms, their mainstream classrooms, at play, at meetings outside the school and even during phone calls (p. 76).

Specifically, Miller's study reports on three "mini-case studies" of three Chinese immigrant students, whom Miller calls Tina, Nora and John. All three students, Miller reports, had more genuine opportunity to use the English language in their intensive English program, where all their classmates were from non-English speaking backgrounds, than they did in their mainstream high school classes. These students found that in the native English speaking environment of mainstream courses, their voices were "neither heard nor understood." "The irony is," writes Miller, "that moving into a mainstream high school actually limited their chances to use English," with Tina and John actually discontinuing to use English save for the classroom (p. 96). In fact, the three students in the study claimed their Anglo-Australian counterparts never spoke to them.

Miller examines two differing views for why these experiences happened to these three students. The first view is that the students themselves chose to be segregated from their Anglo-Australian counterparts. This view, Miller writes, "sits well with the stereotype of Asian students as withdrawn, quiet, and resistant to integration. It also places any social or language problem squarely in the lap of the linguistic minority students themselves, obviating the need for the institutions to do anything 'extra' for the students" (p. 97).

The opposite view, according to Miller, is that the students were "in fact positioned by institutional practices, which include the ways languages and language varieties are valued, the social order that prevails, specific practices relating to academic work, and so on" (p. 97).

Whether by choice or by positioning, Miller claims, the result is that the students' Chinese identities and language became the way for the students to develop and sustain personal identities and relationships, which further causes them to be distant from the dominant Anglo-Australian students. The end result, according to Miller, is that the school system failed to value the students as speakers of a language other than English and that "the lack of opportunities to use English socially at school meant that these students were operating in what was basically a modified foreign-language environment" (p. 97).

In a final study done at the secondary level, Duff (2001) reports on an ethnographic study conducted in a Canadian secondary school housing grades 8 through 12 which had experienced large growth in the number of English as a second language students during the 1990s, especially among students with Asian backgrounds. In fact, Duff reports that "about half of the school's 1300 students were born outside of Canada" (p. 110).

In particular, the study looked at two tenth grade social studies courses, one taught by Pam (17 ESL students) and the other by Bill (8 ESL students). Specifically, the research addressed the following questions: "What are the observed and reported challenges facing ESL students in two SS10 classes, in terms of language, literacy, content, and culture, and how, if at all, are those challenges met?" (p. 111). To answer these two questions, Duff conducted observations once a week for each course, audio- or video-taped individual classes, (which were later transcribed), then individually interviewed both teachers and students. The interviews with the teachers lasted up to an hour and were in addition to the normal interactions that took place between teacher and researcher in the classroom. In addition, Duff conducted "semi-structured" half-hour interviews with individual students during lunch periods or after school was out, interviewing "roughly equal numbers of English-L1 and ESL students" (p. 111).

Duff claims that her study found that if ESL students were to be successful participants in such social studies courses, they needed much more than the normal integrative curriculum required. She writes:

> Not only was a deep knowledge of academic language or textbook content needed to participate effectively in classroom discussions but also needed were a knowledge of popular North American culture, a repertoire of newsworthy current events, an ability to express a range of perspectives on social issues, as well as the ability to enter quick-paced, highly intertextual interactions. Students also needed a great deal of confidence, and ESL students on the whole seemed to lack such confidence and the accompanying sense of entitlement or license to speak about their concerns, backgrounds, issues, and views. (p. 120)

Duff believes that there are three general areas where mainstreamed ESL students need greater intervention and assistance. The first general area is in the area of listening and speaking, since the ESL students claimed to be unable to understand other students in their classes, and had a difficult time understanding the teacher's speech as well, which Duff claims was "readily apparent from observations" (p.121).

Further complicating the issue of listening and speaking were the large number of references to contemporary issues and events which, in spite of a mandated curriculum that was intended to be multicultural, was "plainly Eurocentric and Anglo-American." These references "were common", claims

Duff, "raising the bar for both oral and literate proficiency" (p. 121). Therefore, Duff makes the suggestion that ESL students be encouraged to make greater efforts in suggesting discussion topics. These discussions could then be structured in such a way that they specifically address the needs of ESL students to a greater degree.

The second area that Duff feels needs to be addressed is to pay more overt attention to the structure of texts and to the vocabulary used in those texts in social studies courses, once again more directly addressing the needs of ESL students.

The third area that needs to be addressed is to get ESL students, who Duff claims "possessed a depth of knowledge and critical insight that local students lacked," to overcome their fear of "public humiliation" and to exhibit that knowledge (p. 122).

Duff concludes her article by stating that "ESL students regardless of their proficiency level, motivation to excel academically, or years in Canada remained quite removed from open discussions" (p. 122).

The College/University Level

Of the studies done on the articulation process, the studies done at the college/university level have been the most varied. In Ostler (1980), it was decided, since all students at The University of Southern California's American Language Institute were already participating in mainstream classes in their majors and were thus in contact with other students and instructors in the departments in which they were studying on a daily basis, to ask these students, through the use of a questionnaire, to determine what skills they themselves felt were needed to succeed in academics. Ostler writes that "this questionnaire consisted of fifty-six questions of a biographical and self-evaluating nature, as well as three sentence combining tasks and a paragraph from which two tasks were used to assess summary skills" (p. 490).

The biographical portion "primarily surveyed the population distribution according to native language and country, length of time in the United States and at USC, the number of languages spoken, and units of university work currently being taken" (p. 491).

Overall, Ostler found that the most important skills that the students reported needing were "the abilities to read text books" (90 percent), to "take notes in class" (84 percent), and "ask questions in class" (68 percent) (p. 492). The ability to write research papers and the ability to read academic journals and papers tied at 58 percent. Another primary skill area identified was the ability to write book reviews at 46 percent, with 41 percent reporting that they needed to give talks in class.

In terms of the difference between undergraduates and graduate students, Ostler writes, "Undergraduates indicated a greater need for the skills of taking multiple choice exams, writing laboratory reports, and reading and making graphs and charts. By contrast, graduate students indicated a need to be able to read academic journals and papers, give talks in class and participate in panel discussions, write critiques, research protocols and research papers, discuss issues, and ask questions in class. Only two skills, (1) reading academic papers and journals, and (2) writing research papers, were found to tie the needs of juniors and seniors closer to graduate students than to freshmen and sophomores" (p. 494).

Ostler found a difference "in verbal skills required between making business transactions and those needed in creative language settings." The survey, Ostler sums up, "Focused attention on the need to teach not only reading and writing, but specialized skills such as reading academic journals and papers and writing critiques" as well (p. 499).

In a study designed to "determine (a) what types of experience former ESL students perceived as having contributed most to their language learning while they were in intensive language programs, (b) what qualities of teacher behavior former ESL students perceived as contributing most to their learning, and (c) what types of language use predominated for former ESL students in their academic work and what skills they regarded as easy or difficult for them," (p. 64), Christison & Krahnke (1986) surveyed 80 non-native English speakers who had all completed intensive ESL programs at five different universities and who, at the time of the study, were all enrolled full-time in mainstream academic study. Using open-ended interviews based on a structured questionnaire, the authors found that the use of written discourse was ranked as the most difficult language skill area. Contact with native speakers, such as in social settings or classroom discussions, was considered the most important factor for language improvement. Overall, "Interacting with native speakers was considered the best way to improve their language skills by 65% of the subjects" (p. 69).

Christison & Krahnke's subjects also reported that "80% of their academically related language use was spent in reading and listening (the receptive skills), with only 20% spent in speaking and writing (the productive skills)" (p. 70). According to their subjects' perceptions, speaking and listening to lectures were the two most difficult tasks to perform in academic settings.

The authors conclude from their study that intensive English programs are doing an adequate job. The subjects in their study, they state, "felt that intensive ESL programs provide a good general preparation for academic work." However, they also believe that "the majority did not seem to think that instruction in specific skills, such as writing specific rhetorical types or narrowly defined reading skills, addressed their later needs" (p. 72).

Christison & Krahnke reach several conclusions regarding the implications of their study. "First," they write, "the evidence confirms that some kind of natural interaction using the language being learned is regarded as a major means of learning the language" (p. 75). Their subjects felt, they write, that interacting with native speakers in situations that involve genuine tasks was the main contributor to successful language acquisition. A second conclusion that they reach is that "the receptive skills of listening and reading may have greater importance than are usually attached to them" (p. 76). While this may seem contradictory to their first conclusion, Christison & Krahnke explain this contradiction by writing that "speaking and interaction were valuable for learning the language but that listening and reading were more important in helping them survive in the academic arena" (p. 76). The authors also claim that the study shows that comprehensibility is one of the most important qualities for a language teacher to possess. Finally, the authors conclude that "students can be valuable sources of information on the language learning, socialization, and academic preparation experience" (p. 77).

In another study at the university level, Smoke (1988) investigated perceptions of former ESL students regarding what they were prepared for in their ESL courses and what they later found was required in content area courses. In this study, Smoke "randomly selected 198 ESL students who had completed developmental writing courses between 1980 and 1985" at Hunter College. A questionnaire was mailed or given as an interview to these students. This questionnaire first "asked students if they felt their English skills had improved as a result of ESL courses; 97% believed that they had. However, when asked if they had felt prepared for college courses when they completed remediation, only 18% said yes. 57% responded that they were 'somewhat' prepared and 25% responded that they were not prepared" (p. 13). Smoke then followed up the questionnaire with phone calls and subsequent interviews with 14 students were conducted to find out what specific needs they felt they had.

Students were asked what courses they would add to the present ESL curriculum: 27 percent said pronunciation, 23 percent a speech course, and 24 percent a research paper course. One question also asked students to describe the difficulties they were having in courses that followed the developmental sequence. Ninety two percent indicated "understanding how to read and study from text books," 87 percent "writing research papers," 81 percent answered "talking to professors," 74 percent said "taking notes from lecture classes," and 71 percent marked "answering exam questions" (p. 13). Fifty six percent indicated that they felt nervous when a research paper was required for the class, while 37 percent indicated that they would drop the course.

Smoke states that "the findings of this study indicate that early intervention is necessary if ESL students are to progress and ultimately succeed in college" (p. 14). Her recommendation to "better serve these students" is to "offer combined content-area and language courses." She also recommends that ESL students "take freshman composition immediately upon completion of the developmental writing and reading sequence" (p. 15).

Smoke also found that students take courses in which they can avoid writing research papers. Therefore, she writes, "One way our colleagues could support efforts to better prepare ESL students would be to require some type of writing in every class" (p. 15). The quest for more pronunciation and speech classes is interpreted by Smoke as the students "asking for more participation in college" (p. 15). She concludes that combining content-area and language courses would help those students who have indicated their desire to be able to read textbooks, take notes, and write papers.

Kelley & Sweet (1991) investigated several factors affecting minority language students in a small community college in western Massachusetts. The purpose of the research was, they write, "to find out what is happening at the crucial stage of mainstreaming - what are the factors that come together to influence participation, engagement, and retention of non-native English-speaking students" (p. 2).

The study took place in "a small community college of about 3000 students in western Massachusetts." Kelley & Sweet report:

> It is located in a town which has seen a large influx of Spanish-speaking Puerto Rican families over the last 20 years. Many of the elementary and secondary schools in the community have responded to these changes in

the community through the implementation of transitional bilingual education programs, as well as magnet schools and other innovative programs. However, the community college has a relatively new ESL program and the faculty at the college have little experience in dealing non-native English speaking students. (p. 4)

In order to "accurately capture what happens to these language minority students after they leave the ESL program," the researchers conducted an ethnographic study of the participation of second language speakers in mainstream courses at the community college. In particular, they studied three "Developmental English" classes, "non-credit reading and writing classes which a student must attend if he or she does not receive a satisfactory score on the college's English placement exam" (p. 4). In addition to observations, they also took field notes from every class observation, audio-recorded many classes, interviewed 14 students "at least once each," and "formally interviewed the two participating instructors at various times throughout the semester" (p. 4).

The researchers found that "interaction in the classroom is central because interaction is central to participation and achievement." They continue, "The negotiation involves participation and is critical to learning, but can be very difficult for the language minority student in the college mainstream. A student for whom English is not a first language not only has to deal with differing linguistic norms, but cultural norms as well" (p. 6).

Through analysis of the data collected in the study, the authors state, "Some preliminary patterns have been found which show that some language minority students are not, in fact, participating or experiencing success in the mainstream classes, and which show some reasons why there is a lack of participation. The data show that language minority students who are first-language dominant speak very little in class, if at all. Students are unwilling to read aloud, share their assignments out loud, or even respond to questions from the teacher." Through observation as well as interviewing, it became clear to the researchers that "these students often know the correct answer, or have their homework assignment completed, but lack the confidence to speak aloud in the class. They worry about being 'the only person with an accent' or that the teacher and other students will not understand them" (p. 7).

Kelley & Sweet conclude that untrained teachers who lack experience in dealing with ESL students may misconstrue such students' silence as "poor attitude, lack of interest, or lack of linguistic or cognitive ability." They found that instructors consistently doubted the abilities of these students. "Through data collection, however," they write, "it has become clear that the often implicit norms of classroom participation that are enforced by the instructor limit the opportunities for language minority student success, especially when they are not made explicit" (p. 8). They continue, "Teachers' expectations seem to play an important role in the relationship between students and teacher. English proficiency is often interpreted by instructors as 'intelligence'" (p. 9).

Kelley & Sweet found that students would respond to their teachers' reactions by either by becoming defensive or withdrawing from the class. On the other hand, the participation and success of students in one of the classes studied demonstrated to the researchers that course content and actions on the part of teachers can play an important role in the success of such students. These actions include personalizing the class, incorporating multicultural course content, having well-communicated, high expectations, and explaining "class norms" at the outset of the semester.

Shuck (1995) surveyed students' perceptions of how an intensive English program's writing course prepared them for composition courses at The University of Arizona. All students participating in the survey had attended the UA's Center for English as a Second Language (CESL), where they had 4-5 hours of English-language instruction per day (including a one hour composition course), then had been mainstreamed into classes at UA. Shuck began her study by distributing surveys to all ESL composition instructors in the university's composition program, then subsequently interviewed seven students for a half hour each. At the end of the interviews, the seven students filled out a quantitative questionnaire.

Nearly all of the students had positive comments to make about the intensive English program. They praised their teachers' kindness, helpfulness, and clarity of speaking. They reported that the teachers helped them understand American culture, classroom culture, and the relationship between teacher and student in the United States. They also claimed to have gained improved fluency and listening comprehension in an intensive, but friendly, atmosphere. They also praised teachers for helping them to understand the structures of academic texts and rhetorical strategies. The students, in various ways, all stressed the importance of learning how to revise compositions.

Based on her findings, Shuck makes several suggestions. She suggests that intensive English programs encourage students to read and write more, making the connection between reading and writing, taking into account the different needs and interests of different students. For graduate students, Shuck suggests more specialized readings. She suggests that students be given more time to practice before moving on, introducing them to a wider genre of writing, teaching them how to take in-class exams, and helping them use their time more wisely. She also suggests that students be allowed to take more university courses while still in the intensive English program, and that teachers talk about what future composition classes will be like.

Leki (1999), reports on a single case study of Jan, a student who had immigrated from Poland at age 17 and who was a first-year college student when Leki began her study. Prior to the study, Jan had graduated from an American high school. For her study, either Leki or one of her research assistants held biweekly interviews of roughly an hour each. In addition, they collected class notes, course work, and course handouts. They also carried out interviews with Jan's teachers and observed classes. Ultimately, the study attempted to answer the question "What are the experiences, particularly literacy experiences, of NNES [non-native English-speaking students] at a U.S. University?" (p. 19).

Ultimately, Leki writes, Jan was a "survivor." He had flown directly from his hometown in Poland and "3 days later started as a junior in high school" (p. 22). The high school that Jan attended had different levels of ESL courses. Jan began attending these courses and quickly made his way up to the higher levels. At the same time, Jan was also taking mainstream junior and senior level English courses, which he passed.

While at the university, Leki reports, Jan would only expend effort on activities that he knew he would be tested on or which would be turned in for homework. If Jan was aware that materials would not be tested until a major exam, he would disregard those materials in favor of more pressing concerns, then cram for the test 2 or 3 days prior. In this way, Leki states, Jan "didn't study to understand, only to memorize" (p. 35).

Leki cites several instances where the university system failed Jan. Because of an apparent misunderstanding on the part of the university, Jan had been admitted late and had therefore not been given an orientation to the university. Because of this he had not been advised about several key facts, among them that he could drop courses if he was doing badly in them and that he should work fewer hours than he was accustomed to working. In addition, Jan had no fellow international students to turn to for guidance or advice, and was apparently unable to make new American friends. In addition, the courses that Jan enrolled in as a first year student were all very large, some with literally hundreds of students packed into a large auditorium. This, claims Leki, made it impossible for Jan to ask questions or to let the instructor know when he was confused or unable to keep up with lectures.

Leki also criticizes the system for failing to develop critical thinking skills in Jan, since his assignments included very few extensive writing assignments, rather favoring multiple-choice exams that simply promoted short-term memorization. The greatest failure of the system in Leki's opinion, however, was its failure to provide a "community of peers" to help Jan.

CHAPTER THREE
METHODOLOGY

Introduction

Sevigny (1981) writes that "the task of the qualitative methodologist is to capture what people say and do as a product of how they interpret the complexity of their world. In order to grasp the meaning of a person's behavior, the qualitative researcher seeks to understand social events from the person's point of view - to gain understanding through the participant's perspective" (p. 68). This perspective, writes Sevigny, includes "the informants' predispositions, purposes, assumptions, values, expectations, and attitudes" (p. 66).

In an effort to discover this "participant's perspective," the methodology of ethnography was chosen for the present study. Watson-Gegeo (1988) writes that "ethnography has been greeted with enthusiasm because of its promise for investigating issues difficult to address through experimental research, such as sociocultural processes in language learning, how institutional and societal pressures are played out in moment-to-moment classroom interaction, and how to gain a more holistic perspective on teacher-student interactions to aid teacher training and improve practice" (p. 575).

Continuing, Watson-Gegeo writes, "Ethnographic methods offer us an approach for systematically documenting teaching-learning interactions in rich, contextualized detail with the aim of developing grounded theory (i.e. theory generated from data). The long-term nature of ethnographic research allows for an examination of how teaching and other interactional patterns develop and change over time in a given setting" (pp. 585-586).

Because I was interested in discovering how students' perspectives change over time, that is, as they actually make the transition from an intensive English program to mainstream university courses, ethnography provided the most accessible methodology for this study. Therefore, this chapter begins with a discussion of the nature of ethnographic research, then proceeds with an explicit description of the methodology adopted, which includes the specific questions addressed in each of the interviews conducted.

Ethnography

"Originally developed in anthropology," according to Watson-Gegeo (1988), "to describe the 'ways of learning' of a social group (Heath 1982), ethnography is the study of people's behavior in naturally occurring, outgoing settings, with a focus on the cultural interpretation of behavior" (p. 576). Zaharlick & Green (1991) write that "it is the theoretically driven, systematic approach to the study of everyday life of a social group" (p. 205). Lutz (1981), echoing Geertz (1973), states that "ethnography is a holistic, thick description of the interactive processes involving the discovery of important and recurring variables in the society as they relate to one another, under specific conditions, and as they affect or produce certain results and outcomes in the society" (p. 52).

Spradley (1979) writes that "ethnography is the work of describing a culture. The essential core of this activity aims to understand another way of life from the native point of view. The goal of ethnography, as Malinowski (1922) puts it, is 'to grasp the native's point of view, his relation to life, to realize his vision of his world.' Fieldwork, then, involves the disciplined study of what the world is like to people who have learned to see, hear, speak, think, and act in ways that are different. Rather than studying people, ethnography is learning from people" (p. 3).

Werner & Schoepfle (1987) write, "The ethnographer tries to obtain the knowledge of the natives. This knowledge is rarely, if ever, made fully explicit.

The non-explicit aspects of cultural knowledge can often be inferred from casual remarks that must be clarified by more systematic questioning. The natives, by definition, do not engage in systematic acquisition of knowledge. This more accidental and unsystematic acquisition creates variation from individual to individual. However, the ethnographer must transcend the accidental and replace it with controlled and systematic data illuminating the intra-cultural uniformity and variation of cultural knowledge" (pp. 42-43).

According to Werner & Schoepfle, ethnographic descriptions must closely resemble the original cultural reality. They discuss this resemblance in terms of what they call the "internal" view. "This view," they write, "is never presented in pure form - even the natives may find such a rehash dull. Rather, the internal view must be informed by internal diversity (discrepant views) and by the 'stereo' vision of the ethnographer. This binocular depth perception derives from living, conversing, observing, and writing in the interface between the native culture and the culture of the users of the ethnographic product. The ideal ethnographer studies another culture by bringing external and internal diversity to bear upon an ethnographic problem" (p. 24).

The difference between internal and external views has also been put in terms of *emic* and *etic* distinctions. Watson-Gegeo (1988) writes, "We owe the emic-etic distinction to Pike (1964), who extended the phonetic/phonemic distinction in linguistic meaning to cultural meaning. Pike pointed out that the emic or culturally specific framework used by members of a society/culture for interpreting and assigning meaning to experiences differs in various ways from the researcher's ontological or interpretive framework. . . . An analysis built on emic concepts incorporates the participants' perspectives and interpretations of behavior, events, and situations and does so in the descriptive language they themselves use (Spradley, 1979)" (pp. 579-580).

Ethnography is not, she points out, exclusively emic. "Rather, a carefully done emic analysis precedes and forms the basis for etic extensions that allow for cross-cultural or cross-setting comparisons. . . . The ethnographer first seeks to build a theory of the setting under study, then to extrapolate or generalize from that setting or situation to others studied in a similar way. The comparison must be built on careful emic work" (pp. 580-581).

Watson-Gegeo continues, "Etic analyses and interpretations are based on the use of frameworks, concepts, and categories from the analytic language of the social sciences and are potentially useful for comparative research across languages, settings, and cultures. To be useful in that way, however, etic terms must be carefully defined and operationalized" (p. 580).

There are certain principles orienting ethnography, according to Watson-Gegeo (1988, pp. 577-578). First, ethnography focuses on people's behavior in groups and on cultural patterns in that behavior. Ethnographers are of course interested in individuals, for it is individuals who are observed and interviewed and with whom the ethnographer develops personal relationships. Individual differences are also important for establishing variation in behavior. However, most ethnographic studies are concerned with group rather than individual characteristics because cultural behavior is by definition shared behavior.

Second, ethnography is holistic; that is, any aspect of a culture or a behavior has to be described and explained in relation to the whole system of which it is a part (Diesing, 1971; Firth, 1961).

Third, ethnographic data collection begins with a theoretical framework directing the researcher's attention to certain aspects of situations and certain kinds of research questions. Theory is important for helping ethnographers decide what kinds of evidence are likely to be significant in answering research questions posed at the beginning of the study and developed while in the field (Narroll & Cohen, 1970, 1973; Pelto & Pelto, 1970). If observation is not guided by an explicit theoretical framework, it will be guided only by the observer's "implicit ontology," that is, his or her values, attitudes, and assumptions about 'what sorts of things make up the world [or universe of study], how they are related, and how they act' (Diesing, 1971)."

Regarding the first of these principles, Zaharlick & Green (1991) write that the ethnographer "must consider both the observed patterns of the culture of the specific group under study and the patterns of norms and expectations for engaging in daily life individuals bring to the local situation" (p. 210).

Regarding the second principle, Watson-Gegeo (1988) states that ethnography differs from other forms of qualitative research in its concern with holism and in the way it treats culture as integral to the analysis, not just one of many factors to take into consideration. Zaharlick & Green (1991) state that "in an ethnographic study, an ethnographer will use a holistic perspective to describe the broad context and patterns of life to understand how the parts (pieces of culture) relate to the 'whole' culture. However, while ethnographers are concerned with the 'whole,' they may elect to take a more 'focused' look at particular aspects or elements of everyday life either within a more comprehensive ethnography or as a topic-oriented approach to ethnography" (p. 207).

Regarding the third principle, Zaharlick & Green (1991) write that "the framework provides a place to begin the design of the research. This framework is not used rigidly or to limit what is to be observed or to be explored; rather, the framework forms a basis for making initial decisions about the questions to be asked, the group to be studied, the types of information that are potentially available, the types of data to be collected, and the approaches to analysis of the data that are appropriate" (p. 207).

An ethnographer, they continue, "will bring differing views, methods, theories, and data together to obtain an understanding of the meanings held by participants as reflected in their actions and perceptions. By bringing these views together, that is, by triangulating perspectives, the ethnographer is able to explore and refine the questions that were of interest at the onset of the study and generate questions that could not be anticipated before entry into the 'field.' Thus, ethnographers must continually adapt their questions and plans to the local conditions of the setting as their studies progress (Spradley, 1980)" (p. 209).

Ethnographic research, Watson-Gegeo (1988) writes, "reminds us of the important role of culture in second language teaching and learning and gives us a way of addressing this issue." She continues, "To accomplish the goal of providing a descriptive and interpretive-explanatory account of people's behavior in a given setting, the ethnographer carries out systematic, intensive, detailed observation of that behavior" (p. 577).

According to Werner & Schoepfle (1987) this is accomplished through the combination of both insider and outsider perspectives which "provides deeper insights than are possible by the native alone or an ethnographer alone. The two views, side by side, produce a 'third dimension' that rounds out the ethnographic picture" (p. 63).. "Traditional ethnography," they write, "consists partly of participant observation and partly of conversation or interview. The mix of the two is important" (p. 44).

It is clear, then, that the two approaches complement each other – one is incomplete without the other. Therefore, for the purpose of this study, the methods of data collection consisted of both interviews and observations.

Informants

For the purposes of this study, informants were all chosen from the pool of students enrolled in an intensive English program, hereafter referred to as the IEP, at a medium-sized Midwestern university, hereafter referred to as The University, during the fall semester of 1998. The informants were selected based on their advanced status in the IEP. They were all students who were in their final semester of study at the IEP and were ready to begin study in mainstream university courses, but had not yet begun such courses. These informants were selected from a list of all possible students enrolled in the IEP who fit certain criteria.

Following Bernard (1995, p. 166), the following criteria were used:
1. A good consultant should be articulate.
2. A good consultant should be thoughtful. The ideal person in this position can respond and comment on his or her cultural experience.
3. Good informants are people who you can talk to easily, who understand the information you need, and who are glad to give it to you or get it for you.
4. Good informants are selected for their competence rather than just for their representativeness.

A total of six informants were chosen. Three of the informants were graduate students, three were undergraduate students. The informants ranged in age from 20 to 34 years old. Two of the informants were from South America, two from Asia, one from Africa, and one from the Middle East. None of the six informants shared the same first language or the same major. Several of the informants had wide work experiences, while the youngest had no work experience at all. Three of the informants were married, while only one of the informants, the oldest, had any children.

The Intensive English Program and The University

The Intensive English Program is part of the Department of English at The University. Its main function is to prepare students for academic study at The University. It is designed to help students improve their spoken English, introduce them to the culture of the United States, and give them special training in technical writing and research skills.

In the IEP, classes are small, seldom having more than 10 students. They provide classes in the areas of writing, reading, listening, conversation, and grammar. In addition, the IEP has a language laboratory for listening and pronunciation work. There are a total of three semesters throughout the year for students to take classes, fall, spring, and summer. Some students are also able to take mainstream classes while completing their IEP courses.

The University bills itself as "a comprehensive, publicly assisted institution of higher education whose mission is to provide excellent education." In a promotional brochure, The University claims to offer "more varied academic programs than the small liberal arts college while providing a more personalized educational experience than may be found at a large research-oriented university." The University has an enrollment under 20,000 students and offers 140 major and minor areas at the associate, baccalaureate, master's, and doctoral levels. It is primarily a residential community.

Interviews

The primary means of data gathering for this study was through informant interviews. All Interviews were held in the researcher's office located in the IEP. This provided an easily accessible meeting place for the students. It was also a relatively quiet place where interviews could be tape recorded easily and without distraction. All interviews occurred at the convenience of the informants.

As Spradley (1979) observes, "When an ethnographer and informant meet together for an interview, both realize that the talking is supposed to go somewhere. The informant only has a hazy idea about this purpose; the ethnographer must make it clear" (p. 59). Therefore, informants were given a complete description of the nature of the project. A rationale for why certain types of questions were asked was also given.

For these interviews, primary interest was in what Werner & Schoepfle (1987) call "open, epistemic (knowledge seeking) interviews." The range of these interviews extended "from relative openness, especially in the initial phases of a series of interviews, to relatively closed interviews with prepared interview schedules, question frames, or completely precoded or closed questions" (p. 307).

Following Spradley (1979), the following succession of questions was asked:

1. Grand Tour Questions: a grand tour question simulates an experience many ethnographers have when they first begin to study a cultural scene: "Would you like a grand tour of the place?"
2. Mini Tour Questions: mini tour questions respond to grand tour questions. They offer almost unlimited opportunities for investigating smaller aspects of experience. Mini tour questions are identical to grand tour questions except that they deal with a much smaller unit of experience.
3. Example Questions: example questions take some single act or event identified by the informant and ask for an example. This type of question can be woven throughout almost any ethnographic interview.
4. Experience Questions: experience questions merely ask informants for any experiences they have had in a particular setting.

Interview Schedule

Initial interviews were held before the end of the fall semester of 1998, the semester in which the study began. Subsequent interviews were held at intervals of three to four weeks, depending on the availability of informants, with the final interviews held either immediately prior to or immediately after the end of the spring semester of 1999. Class observations were held immediately after the mid-semester break. Following is a more complete description of the interviews and observations, including specific questions asked.

The Initial Interview

The purpose of the initial interview, which was conducted in two parts, was to clarify the nature of the study and to explain to the informants the risks and benefits involved. Informants were advised that the interviews would be tape recorded and that after the interview, a transcription of relevant parts of each tape would be made. Informants were also told that their names would not be attached to the transcription.

Risks were explained to them, which included the loss of time spent in the interview which could otherwise be spent studying. Benefits were also explained to the informants, which included helping them gain insight into the processes they were experiencing as they made the transition from the IEP to mainstream university classes, as well as helping the IEP and intensive English programs in general. They were also informed that their names would not appear in any publication or presentation of the research. A second purpose of the initial interview was to help make informants comfortable with the study, so that data would be more natural and complete.

This initial interview was based on a set of questions that had been developed prior to the interview. The first section of the interview explored general information, such as the informants' first languages, languages of the home and school, and descriptions of each informant's culture. Also explored was each informant's English language learning background, attempting to discover when the informants first began to learn English, how many years of English they had been taught, what form that teaching had taken, what attitudes they had during their previous English learning experiences, and what experiences they had had with standardized language assessment tests.

The second part of the initial interview was designed to inquire about each informant's present language learning experience, including questions about informants' attitudes toward and motivation for learning English. Also investigated was the support that informants were getting from family members and friends. Questions were also asked about the strategies that informants had used or were using to learn English, as well as questions about the extra-curricular activities that they were engaging in that could help them learn English.

In the final section of the interview, informants were surveyed regarding their perception of their entrance into mainstream university courses, attempting to determine what areas were causing the most apprehension and what areas the informants felt they had the greatest ability in. Informants were also asked about their perceptions of how and when they would use English in the future.

Questions from the initial interview included the following:
1. What is your first language?
2. What language(s) did you speak at home while growing up? At school?
3. How old were you when you first started to learn English?
4. How would you describe the type of classes you took to learn English?
5. What was your attitude toward learning English at that time?
6. Have you ever taken the TOEFL? GRE?
7. What is your attitude toward learning English now?
8. Does your family encourage you to learn English?
9. What strategies do you use to learn English?
10. What kinds of extra-curricular activities do you engage in?
11. How much interaction do you have with native speakers?
12. What areas of study cause you the most apprehension?
13. What do you think are your strongest language abilities?
14. What are your long-term goals in learning English?
15. What do you think you will use English for in the future?

The Second Interview

This series of interviews, which were conducted about three weeks into the spring semester, began by asking the informants to name and describe each of the mainstream university courses that they were now taking. Informants were encouraged to go through their schedules, class by class, and to detail what they were encountering in each of the classes, especially as it related to their use of English. Special attention was given to informants' viewpoints on vocabulary. Also, attention was given to the specific language areas (i.e., speaking, listening, etc.) that were presenting the largest obstacles for the informants. Informants were also asked to describe surprising aspects of their mainstream classes.

Specific questions included the following:
1. What specific courses are you presently taking?
2. What are those classes like in general?
3. What aspects of the class have given you the most trouble?
4. What aspects do you find the easiest to deal with?
5. What kinds of notes have you taken for each of these classes?
6. Do you ask questions in your classes? Why or why not?
7. What experiences have you had with vocabulary in these classes?
8. How have you dealt with vocabulary problems?
9. What language areas have given you the most trouble?
10. What language areas have been the easiest to deal with?
11. How much time have you spent studying for your classes?
12. How much time have you spent reading for your classes?
13. How would you describe your different instructors' teaching styles?
14. Are you getting help from anyone? If so, who?
15. What surprising aspects of the class have you encountered?

The Third Interview

The third set of interviews was conducted immediately before informants were to take midterm examinations or right after they had taken them. The interviews began once again with informants being asked to review each of the mainstream university courses that they were taking and to describe the experiences that they had had in those courses. Once again, informants were asked about the issues of vocabulary, asking questions in class, and about note taking. Attention was also given to the question of how background knowledge in specific areas affected each class and to the amount of time spent reading. Also surveyed was informants' interaction with their instructors and classmates. In addition, individualized questions were asked regarding specific areas mentioned in the previous set of interviews.

Specific questions during this set of interviews included the following:
1. How much time are you spending on each class?
2. How does the size of the class affect your learning?
3. How much research have you had to do for your classes?
4. How much reading have you had to do for your classes?
5. How would you describe your relationship with your instructor?
6. How would you describe your different instructors' teaching styles?
7. How do you think different teaching styles affect you?
8. Are you doing any group work? If so, could you please describe the group work?
9. Are you making any presentations in class? If so, could you please describe them?
10. Does this course meet the expectations you had at the beginning of the semester?
11. At this point in the semester, have you made the progress that you expected to make? Why or why not?
12. If you could go back and do the first half of the semester again, what would you do differently?
13. Looking back, how do you think the IEP could have prepared you better for mainstream classes?

The Class Observations

Class observations were held after the third interview. These observations were conducted to independently confirm statements made by the informants regarding their courses. Courses chosen for observation were based on previous discussions held with informants in an effort to verify some of the more interesting statements made by them. Therefore, courses where the informants were having the most difficulty or had the most questions were chosen. For the purposes of these observations, the researcher first had informants consult with the instructors of these courses, asking for permission for a visitor to attend their classes. After permission was granted, the researcher and informant consulted to determine which particular day would be the best for observation, in this way avoiding days with tests, etc. During the actual observation, the researcher sat in the back of the class when possible so as not to interrupt the natural flow of the class. Notes were taken during the observations which were then used to form the foundation of the fourth interview.

The Fourth Interview

The fourth series of interviews was conducted as soon as possible after the classroom observation visits. The focus of the first half of the interview was on the class observed and the things that the researcher observed about the class. Specific questions based on each classroom observation were asked for each informant. In the second half of the interview, more general questions were asked of the classes being taken. Of particular interest here was the amount of time informants were spending on group work, as well as time studying in general. Also of interest was finding out what extra efforts informants were making to ensure that their learning was more effective.

Specific questions for the fourth series of interviews included the following:

1. Are you doing group work in your courses?
2. If so, what kinds of group work are you expected to do?
3. What problems, if any, have you experienced with group work?
4. Do you feel that group work is different in your culture?
5. What aspects of American academic culture do you think are different?
6. What kinds of experiences have you had with tests in your courses?
7. How does time affect your study?
8. How is technology affecting your study?
9. Are you asking questions in your classes?

10. Does reading different types of texts affect your study?
11. Are you getting any extra help with your courses? If so, where?
12. What things do teachers do that make the class easier for you?
13. Have you taken courses similar to the ones you are now taking? How does that affect your study?
14. How are you adapting your behavior to make your learning more successful?
15. What strategies are you using in your classes right now?

The Final Interview

   The final set of interviews was conducted either immediately prior to the end of the semester or immediately after the end of the semester. In addition to asking the informants to recount their experiences in each class, this series of interviews also asked informants to focus on their performance and behavior over the semester. Informants were asked to detail how they would have acted differently if they were given the chance, and how they could have better prepared themselves. Informants were also asked to explain how they planned to change their learning behavior in the future.

   Specific questions for the final set of interviews included the following:

1. What experiences did you have with tests?
2. What experiences did you have with group work?
3. What experiences did you have with presentations?
4. Were you getting help from any one? If so, where?
5. Has your learning style changed over the course of the semester? If so, how?
6. What strategies that you used were the most helpful?
7. What do you see as the biggest hurdle that you had to overcome over the course of the semester?
8. Overall, what do you perceive as the biggest differences between IEP classes and mainstream classes?

9. What could the IEP have done differently to make your semester more productive?
10. If you could go back and change your behavior over the semester, what would you have done differently?
11. How do you plan to change your behavior in the future?

Records

Once the interviews were completed, a permanent record was made. An ethnographic record consists of field notes, tape recordings, pictures, artifacts, and anything else which documents the cultural scene under study. Spradley (1979) writes that "both native terms and observer terms will find their way into the field notes. The important thing is to carefully distinguish them. The native terms must be recorded verbatim. Failure to take these first steps along the path to discovering the inner meaning of another culture will lead to false confidence that we have found what the natives know." He continues, "The ethnographer must make a verbatim record of what people say. Whether recording things people say in natural contexts or in more formal ethnographic interviews. The investigator's tendency to translate continues to operate" (p. 73).

Werner & Schoepfle (1987) write, "A careful comparison of field data from different sources is possible only if the ethnographer approaches fieldwork with a carefully designed data management and retrieval system. That is, statements of protocols about the same or similar events must be easily accessible in the ethnographic record" (p. 64).

For the purposes of this study, two major records were kept: a journal and transcripts. Each of these records is detailed below.

The Journal

Spradley (1979) writes that an ethnographer should "always keep a journal. Like a diary, this journal will contain a record of experiences, ideas, fears, mistakes, confusions, breakthroughs, and problems that arise during fieldwork. A journal represents the personal side of fieldwork; it includes reactions to informants and the feelings you sense from others" (p. 76).

For Spradley, the journal is an "expanded account." He writes, "As soon as possible after each field session, the ethnographer should fill in details and recall things that were not recorded on the spot. The key words and phrases jotted down can serve as useful reminders to create the expanded account. When expanding, different speakers must be identified and verbatim statements included." This allows, he explains, for "analysis and interpretation. One can think on paper" (p. 75).

Werner & Schoepfle (1987) write that the journal should include both "external observations" and "internal observations." External observations include observations about the surroundings. Internal observations include "introspections, feelings about the work, and feelings about the surroundings" (p. 273).

Additionally, Werner & Schoepfle write that a journal should be used to record such things as "observations of changing field relations and observations on the changing direction of one's research. As a method for safeguarding a culture's internal view, then, any research design, however beautifully conceived originally, may in practice require major adjustments, or simply fine-tuning, in order to adequately reflect the internal point of view. These adjustments or research goals, whether large or small, should also find their way into the journal's pages" (p. 273). The journal also has a mnemonic function, they claim, helping the ethnographer to remember important information.

For the purposes of this study, following Bernard (1995), the journal was divided up into two parts. Each interview day was represented by a double page of the journal. The pages on the left hand side were used to plan what was to be done on a given interview day. The facing pages were used to recount what actually was done that day. Notes on issues to be discussed and specific questions to be asked were also recorded in the journal. Also included were target dates for when interviews were to be conducted, when transcripts were to be completed, and when a written product was expected. In addition, short profiles of each of the informants, along with the informants' schedules, were kept in the journal.

Transcripts

In addition to journal records, pertinent sections of tape recordings were transcribed and coded. As Spradley (1979) points out, tape-recorded interviews, when fully described, represent one of the most complete expanded accounts. Tape recordings represent the language of the informant, not the ethnographer.

These transcriptions must then be coded. For the purposes of this study, transcripts were coded using a modified version of the Outline of Cultural Materials (see Bernard, 1995).

CHAPTER FOUR
CASE STUDIES OF SIX FORMER IEP STUDENTS

Introduction

This study followed six international students at a medium-sized Midwestern university, referred to as The University, as they made the transition from an intensive English program, referred to as the IEP, to mainstream university courses. The following section provides case studies of these six students. All names have been changed and identifying characteristics have been altered or omitted to protect confidentiality.

Three undergraduate students and three graduate students were chosen for this study. Each of the six informants was chosen on the following basis: that at the beginning of the study they had been long-term students at the IEP, had reached the advanced levels of the IEP, were all in the final semester of study at the IEP, and were therefore preparing to make the transition to mainstream university courses, but had not yet done so.

The initial interview, which was conducted in two parts, took place while the informants were still attending the IEP. This initial interview was conducted to provide background information on each of the six informants, as well as to provide a foundation on which to build ethnographic questions and to provide a comparative basis for the different informants. Informants were then interviewed at intervals of approximately three weeks throughout the following semester, during which all six informants began attending mainstream university courses. These subsequent interviews were designed to determine what factors had changed in the classroom setting, how informants' perceptions of their learning process had changed in the intervals between interviews, what actions, both on their part and the part of their instructors, had helped or hindered the learning process, and finally, what suggestions informants had for improvement of the IEP.

Samory
"I should grab on to everything I can."

The Background Interview

At the time of his first interview, Samory was a highly personable, friendly twenty-four year old male graduate student from a small francophone country in West Africa. Although his undergraduate degree, which he received in 1993, was in sociology, he was at The University to study natural resources. Samory attributed this interest in natural resources to his first job, which he began in January 1993. He worked at this job, which was sponsored by a large American university, for a total of three and a half years. His main task was "to do research on traditional national resources management practices from a sociological standpoint." After this experience he changed jobs and began to work for an economic development agency. In 1997, he won a scholarship from this agency to study in the United States.

Samory's first language was a West African language. Both his mother and father spoke this language in the home. As a child, he also picked up one other West African language. Since the people of his village spoke one or the other of the two languages as the language of the home, he related, if he wanted to converse with friends and neighbors, it was necessary to learn to speak both languages.

Samory was also fluent in French, which he began to learn for the first time at the age of six when he attended his first day of elementary school. Classes, he declared, were taught entirely in French "from the first moment." He stated that it was difficult to learn French, particularly since he spoke his native language at home with his mother and father.

Samory's English language learning began when he was in high school. There, in addition to his West African teachers, he also had a Canadian teacher. He stated that at that point, he had only learned "basic stuff." It was not until he won the scholarship in 1997, he maintained, that he began to study English seriously.

After winning the scholarship in 1997, he studied "for five or six months" at a center for English as a second language at his country's main university. There, he related, he learned speaking, reading, writing, listening, and grammar. However, he stated that his teachers were all from his native country and "had a hard time teaching American English" because they themselves had studied primarily British English. Added to this was the fact that the books and tapes in the program had been donated by an American university. His teachers at the center had a very difficult time teaching with these American-centered materials, he claimed.

During the period when he was working at his first job, he had American coworkers. While he spoke primarily French to them, he said that he had had some experiences speaking English with them. During this period, he also had an American girlfriend who "wrote letters and spoke a little in English" to him. He claimed that this experience was helpful when he first went to the center to learn English, since he was able to begin at a higher level than the others who began studying at the center at the same time as he.

After learning enough "basic skills," Samory came to the United States in December 1997. At that time, he began to attend English classes at a university different from The University. There, he attended an intensive English program from January to August 1998. He stated that he learned all skill areas "communicatively." He said that it was "really intensive," which he believed was "the best way to learn English." The instructors in this program also used videotapes, he related, which he found highly interesting and which he felt helped build up his listening ability. At the time, he did not feel very confident in his English abilities. However, his teachers assured him that he had the potential to be successful in his graduate studies, which served to give him confidence to continue on.

Samory felt that the best way to learn a language at the beginning stages was to study English intensively, and to "say nothing but English." He felt that when a student reaches a point of confidence, perhaps at the high-intermediate level, they should switch to regular university classes, which would in turn help them learn English by "making them more familiar with the vocabulary of their major." He believed that a good language learner must concentrate and pay attention. He also felt that students should "be near the teacher" and should be "active" in learning. "Students," he stated, "should put themselves into the right position."

Samory saw a value in learning English, especially when trying to find a job in his home country. His past experiences had proven this to him, he claimed. At one point in his working career at the economic development agency, he applied to be a project administrator with the agency. He stated that he had the experience and training necessary to do the job, but he "didn't know how to speak English." The other candidate for the job did not have the experience or training, but did speak English. In the end, the other person was given the job. The explanation given to Samory was that it was easier and quicker to train the other person in the job skills necessary than it was to teach Samory to speak English.

A second such experience came when applying for a Peace Corps administration position. Once again, he had the experience and training, but the interview was to be conducted in English. He went to the interview but was essentially unable to communicate with the interviewers. Once again, he was not given the job. He asserted that he had all of the qualifications but one: he couldn't speak English.

Samory's perception of learning English was that with a master's degree and a knowledge of English he could "get a job, a good job" after returning to his home country. In virtually any position that he would seek, he stated, he would need to know English, so that he could read such things as letters and memos, and would need to speak English to attend conferences and seminars, both of which, he stated, are generally held in English.

His short-term goals were primarily to study for his master's degree, to pass his classes, and to do well, if possible. He stated that he wanted to be "more active, to make more friends," and to take advantage of the opportunity to meet people in the United States. However, he stated that he had not found it easy to make American friends.

His long-term goals included being able to communicate fluently and easily. He also wanted to encourage people in his country to study English and to encourage the teaching of English there in a more communicative manner. For the long-term learning of English, he planned to take books, CDs, and tapes back with him to study. He also planned to make a point of traveling to English-speaking countries. After returning home, he hoped to obtain a job where he could "use English," most likely at "some international agency, such as the Peace Corps or UNICEF." He stated that whether or not he could use English on the job would be a factor in his job choice.

Samory's perception of the United States, before his arrival, was that America was "a wonderland" and indeed, he said, there were many things here that they did not have in his home country. He was especially impressed with the large libraries and the availability of computers. But he stated that he was now "seeing both sides" and that it was different from what he expected.

He stated that he was trying to understand American culture, but that he felt he would never completely understand it. He attempted to read as much about American culture as he could before coming to America, as well as discussing America with his American coworkers. He felt that he did learn some of the basics, which helped him a great deal when first coming to America. However, he felt that there was still a tremendous amount to learn.

Samory claimed that he did not experience culture shock when he first came to the United States, mostly because he was used to living away from home for his job. Additionally, he stated that he was "too busy to think about culture shock." He also felt that difficulties are a natural part of life, that "there are always good things and bad things about any situation."

In his daily life, he tried to talk to his American landlord and his family, because he was comfortable talking to them. With them, he stated, he was trying to learn about American culture "naturally." However, his primary source of information about America was from other people from his home country who had been studying at The University longer than he.

He also liked to go out to local nightclubs for fun and tried to speak English with the people there. He also reported that he wrote letters and email messages to his friends in America. He felt that he had improved more than the other people from his home country who had come before him, especially in regards to writing. He also read the newspaper daily and was trying to read some novels, although he was generally too busy.

Samory rated his writing ability as his strongest skill area, with reading coming in second. Reading and writing in the classroom, he claimed, didn't alarm him. He rated his listening ability as third and his speaking ability as fourth. He stated that he felt his speaking ability was weak, in spite of the assurance that he had received from his instructors.

He rated himself as having a relatively good ability to learn languages, but was still not terribly confident. He rated his library skills as good, though he felt that the library was "very big" and that he still had some problems mastering the library's computer system. His only previous experience with computers, he related, had been a laptop computer given to him to use for his first job back in his home country, which he had had to learn to use by himself through trial and error.

Samory felt that his note taking ability was good and that his critical thinking skills were relatively good. He rated his questioning ability as "so-so." Overall, he felt that a good language learner was someone who seeks out people to talk to, asking them about their culture, and someone who is confident, but also sits down and studies the language as well.

The Second Interview

The second interview with Samory was conducted approximately three weeks into the spring semester. The primary goal of this interview was to find out what was happening to Samory in his classes. Samory stated that in addition to his classes, he had been attending the Speech Pathology Department's speech lab for pronunciation instruction. He was taking three courses, all at the graduate level: Soil Resources, Environmental Economics, and Computer Applications in Natural Resources.

Samory stated that his Soil Resources class was an interesting class, but that he had been having some problems. He felt that he had "no background" in this field. This, he felt, put him at a great disadvantage. Because he had studied sociology as an undergraduate, he had never had any classes in anything remotely connected to soil. The only class in his educational background that was somewhat related to soil was in junior high school when he took a physical geography class. The other people in the class, he remarked, seemed to have more of a background in soil; most of them had studied something about soil before. In fact, he claimed, virtually everyone in the class was an undergraduate natural resources major, so he felt that he was at a decided disadvantage in this class when compared to his classmates.

Samory stated that a lot of the vocabulary in the class he simply didn't know, especially the specialized vocabulary of soil resources. The teacher, he felt, explained the material at the level of the rest of the class, not down to his level, since he was "the only one without the proper background." He stated that he did inform the teacher beforehand that he did not possess the background that the others had. The instructor had made it clear that he was available and willing to give extra help if needed, however. Samory also stated that he was willing to go to the instructor to ask for help. In fact, the instructor had already loaned him two extra books. Samory reported that he had also sought help from his friends. This class had a lot of homework, as well as a once-a-week lab that he was required to attend.

Samory stated that it bothered him that he didn't understand "everything." He felt that he "would like to understand everything." He felt that he came to The University "to learn and to better myself." He believed that he "should grab on to everything I can."

Samory stated that he liked his Environmental Economics class. He felt more comfortable with the vocabulary of this class because he had read some books previously about the subject. The instructor seemed to cover more economics than environment, however, which concerned him a little. He felt that this was in conflict with what he and the rest of the class were interested in, since they were all natural resource majors. He felt that the balance was not what he wanted. At that point, he stated, the balance was about seventy percent economics, thirty percent environment. He stated that he would like the balance to be about fifty-fifty.

Once again, the teacher was helpful and available, Samory said. He stated that he was comfortable talking to the instructor, who was very clear in his expectations. He gave outlines and handouts of what was expected, as well as suggestions for topics of papers.

Samory's Computer Applications class was an independent study course. It was taught by the same person who was teaching him Soil Resources, which he found very helpful. In this course, he and the instructor worked together to detail land changes of a local township between 1965 and 1992. Samory had to first collect the data and then input the data into the computer. The data had to then be digitalized. At that point, he was still in the data gathering stage.

The major problem for this course was that another person was supposed to teach him how to use the software necessary to complete the analysis. However, at this point, that person didn't know the software either; therefore, she had to learn how to operate the software, then teach him how to use it. In the meantime, he had to begin to do the research and data gathering to complete the project.

Samory stated that he liked the one-to-one style of this course, but the technical skills required of him concerned him greatly. He said that he had no formal training in computers; the only knowledge that he possessed had been gathered through his own experiences, most of which came from learning on his own in a hit-and-miss fashion. In other words, he maintained, he might know how to perform certain functions, but even if he knew how to perform the functions, he didn't know what terms to use for those functions.

Overall, at this point, Samory felt overwhelmed by time. He claimed that he had no chance for anything but study. He stated that he had had no problems with listening, speaking or writing thus far. However, reading was a major problem. He felt that it was not "reading" itself that had given him problems, but rather that he simply had too much to read. He asserted that he was having a hard time keeping up. In addition, there was the problem of the specialized vocabulary of Soil Resources, which he had no background in. This contributed to the slowing down of his reading. This, he perceived, was his biggest obstacle. He felt that this semester would be the most challenging of his graduate school career.

He also stated that he was surprised that no one in class was asking questions. In his home country, he claimed, people asked questions very frequently. He maintained that he liked to ask questions, but felt uncomfortable asking questions in class because no one else was asking questions. This caused a dilemma for him, since he didn't want to be "guilty" of not asking questions and taking every advantage that he could during his period of study in America.

The Third Interview

The third interview with Samory took place prior to spring break, during which time Samory was taking midterms, which in his major were taken somewhat earlier than other majors. He stated that classes were going well at this point.

Samory related that, once again, time was his biggest problem. He said that he had a problem finishing his Environmental Economics midterm in the allotted time. However, the instructor of the class was "kind," since the other members of the class also had problems finishing, and gave the students in the class extra time to finish the midterm. He stated that he gave answers that he knew were wrong to some of the questions because he did not have enough time to answer the questions correctly. He stated that he answered the questions with what he knew were wrong answers because of the lack of time. He was obviously bothered greatly by this. However, he asserted that this had been a good experience. He also stated that he felt he would have to change his attitude toward tests in the future and go in more prepared.

The balance of the Environmental Economics class, according to Samory, was much better at that point, so he and his classmates were much happier. He realized now that the instructor intended that the beginning of the course be more heavily about economics and that they would move more to natural resources later in the semester. He didn't understand this at the beginning, he stated, but now he expressed understanding. He stated that he found that he was not very interested in this class. He planned to return to his home country to work in land resource management, not economics. He felt that if a class was not specifically about land resource management, he was not interested in it, and, more importantly, claimed that he "cannot understand it." In his economics class, the instructor discussed such things as waste management, but he was only interested in sustainable development. In his country, pollution was not the biggest problem; "there are many other bigger problems that need to be dealt with first," he stated. Therefore, if the discussion was not in this specific area, it didn't keep his interest, which he asserted made his class performance suffer.

Samory felt "embarrassed" about his classes at this point. He was trying to make more effort to find out what classes were about before taking them. He felt that many of his classes "won't be useful to me in the future." The problem, he stated, was that there were simply not enough classes in his program that fit his particular interests.

He related that the work load for the Environmental Economics class was "O.K." The reading assignments and the projects were also fine. His only major problem was in taking tests for the course. He asserted that he got good grades on his homework, even though "it is not easy." One problem that he did have was that all examples were taken from the context of the United States, which he felt were harder for him to understand than for his classmates. He stated, however, that this was understandable, since the situation in the United States was what the teacher understood. It was not easy for him to understand these examples, however. He had to do extra things on his own to understand, which once again took up more of his time and put added strain on him. Additionally, he felt that even if he understood, he wouldn't necessarily be able to apply the examples to his own situation in the future since the two countries were "just too different."

The Soil Resources class, according to Samory, had been "a real experience" since it was the first time that he had ever taken such a course. He stated that he liked the class, even though it was hard for him to understand, given his lack of background in the field. He felt that what he was learning was interesting and would help him in the future, since he needed "a basic knowledge about soil," even if he "won't practice everything." He stated that he wouldn't be "one hundred percent a technician," but was nevertheless interested in learning about the techniques covered in the class. In the future, he planned to do research in analysis about land management and would be taking a course in geographical information systems during the fall semester; therefore, he felt that he needed the skills learned from his Soil Resources class for that class. In other words, he had come to realize that "this course will actually be somewhat useful."

Samory stated that vocabulary was still a problem for him because of his lack of background in the field. Currently, he was trying to understand the essential parts, not "everything, like I did before." He was focusing on the key concepts that he had to know in order to go on to future classes. Therefore, he was primarily "reading for understanding." He stated that it was not easy for him to memorize the vocabulary he needed. He said that he was "not intelligent anymore." He was just doing his best to understand more and more. He stated that understanding the concepts was the most important thing for him to do at this point in time. He stated that he had no problem with the homework, when he had enough time to do it, and restated that the lack of background was the worst part.

In his Computer Applications class, Samory was not going as fast as expected. As he explained during his second interview, he was supposed to be working with a person who was to teach him how to use the software needed for the project; however, she had still not finished studying how to use the software, which left Samory asking, "How can I start?" He was therefore forced to wait for her to complete her work before he was able to begin his. He stated that he hoped to start immediately after spring break. He feared that he would end up doing most of the work at the end of the semester, which worried him because that would be his busiest time. He stated that the project would not be as large as initially anticipated. He was working one-to-one with the teacher for this class, however, so the teacher understood his dilemma, which served to make things easier on Samory.

Overall, at this point, Samory was spending a lot of time going to the library and doing extra reading for his classes. This was in addition to all the reading he had to do from his textbooks. Reading, he said, "takes a lot of time." It was necessary to do much reading, he related, especially in his Economics class. The Soil Resources instructor, he reported, had made notes for the students to follow, with key concepts highlighted; therefore, if he didn't have enough time to read everything, he was able to determine what parts were the most important to read and to concentrate on those parts. In the Economics class, however, he had ten chapters that he had to read. He stated that "even a fast reader would take a lot of time to get through that," but that he was "not a fast reader." Also, some of his homework, he declared, had taken a lot of time to complete.

For the Soil Resources laboratory class, Samory had to work with a partner. He stated that this was the first time for him to work in a laboratory setting and that he had "never done experiments before." He said that the lab work had been getting easier as the semester progressed, although it was "still not easy." The problem, he maintained, was to interpret the reactions. It was easy, he felt, to follow the instructions, but it was hard to interpret the results. Once again, he blamed this on his lack of background in the field and lack of experience in the laboratory setting.

Samory stated that this lack of background in the field had also affected his questioning ability in class. He stated that he didn't ask too many questions in the Soil Resources class because he didn't "know what to ask." This was in opposition to the Environmental Economics class, where he felt that he had a stronger background based on previous reading, and where he felt he had no problem asking questions.

Another problem, Samory claimed, was that he was not used to sharing work with other people or asking others for help, since he was rarely, if ever, required to do collaborative work as a student back in his home country. However, he reported that he had recently begun to discuss his homework with friends before doing his homework. This, he felt, had benefited him greatly and he planned to continue to do so in the future.

Samory declared that he didn't feel like he had made the progress that he wanted. He thought that he needed to "provide more effort." He stated that he felt "stuck someplace right now." Because he believed that he wasn't getting what he needed in the Environmental Economics class, he felt discouraged toward that class. And in Soil Resources, despite liking the class and realizing that some aspects of what he had been learning would be useful for him in the future, his lack of background had held him back. In retrospect, Samory stated that he should have put more effort into his classes by doing more reading and trying to understand the key concepts "right from the beginning of the semester." However, he declared that he was confident that the rest of the semester would be better because he would be motivated to get better grades.

The Classroom Observation

The classroom observation for Samory was of his Soil Resources class, which took place in a medium-sized classroom which was physically divided up into two parts, with desks taking up the front half of the classroom and laboratory tables taking up the back half of the classroom. There were approximately 20 students in the class, taking up virtually all of the available seats. Samory sat near the front of the class, close to where the instructor stood during the class.

During the initial part of the class, the instructor handed back a test that the students in the class had taken during the previous class session. The instructor went through the test, essentially question by question. During this period, some the students in the class asked for clarification about certain questions, and some of the students challenged the instructor about how he had marked the test. The instructor appeared willing to answer all of the questions and to address any discrepancies that had occurred in his grading. During this time, Samory did not ask any questions or make any comments about the test. He did, however, periodically lean over to the person sitting next to him, apparently asking for clarification of the explanation that the instructor had given.

After the discussion of the examination was finished, the instructor began a lecture, based on a series of slides. The instructor addressed each slide in turn, lecturing about each one. He would occasionally stop lecturing and ask a question or two. On almost every occasion that he asked a question, however, no one in the class volunteered an answer and the instructor would end up answering the question himself.

During the lecture, all the students in the class took out an identical packet of materials, following along with the materials as the instructor lectured. Samory wrote some notes in this packet, though not very often. On two separate occasions, he also looked over to the packet of the same person sitting next to him, who pointed to a spot in the notes as if to tell Samory which point in the notes the instructor was referring to at that point. This person seemed very much at ease helping Samory.

After the end of the lecture based on the slides, the instructor left several minutes for discussion. However, when prompted by questions from the instructor, very few of the students responded. Therefore, the instructor ended up filling in the remaining time by himself with what amounted to a mini-lecture.

The Fourth Interview

This interview took place immediately after the classroom observation, just after Samory had gotten back his Soil Resources test. The test itself was divided up into three parts: multiple choice questions, math questions, and essay questions. He stated that he did well on the math and essay sections, but very poorly on the multiple choice questions. He stated that he felt that he did not do well on multiple choice tests. He felt that he was not used to that style, since he was not tested in that style when he was young. He asserted that the first time he ever took a multiple choice exam was when he took the TOEFL test. He claimed never to have taken a multiple choice test in his home country. The problem, he felt, was with the data. He stated that he had a hard time memorizing data, since that was something that he had never had to do previously. Therefore, studying for this type of test was difficult for him.

A further problem, maintained Samory, was that he felt that he didn't have the background knowledge that he needed for this class. He stated that he was only taking the class for "basic knowledge," and that he was "a sociologist, not a technician." He felt that he "will never be a technician," so he didn't see the real importance of this class. Therefore, he found it hard to memorize the technical language and details he would need to do well on the multiple choice questions.

While no one had really asked any questions during the class observed, Samory declared that many of the students in the class usually did ask many questions when the instructor lectured. He stated that this was because the other students in the class had a better understanding of the subject than he and knew "what the teacher is talking about," because they had a "stronger background" than he.

Samory felt that none of the students answered the teacher's questions during the slide lecture because they either didn't know the answer or they just didn't want to answer, if they did know the answer. He stated that this was normal for this class. He stated that "people just don't want to talk. Many people don't want to answer the question because the answer is obvious."

Samory related that after the test, he went to talk to the instructor, who told him that there was hope for improvement of his grade. The instructor told him that he could complete a special project, based on one of the upcoming lectures. The instructor asked Samory to do an extra credit paper about one of these subjects. Samory stated that he had decided to do a paper on soil erosion control in his home country, since he already had a series of slides and pictures on the subject. The instructor was allowing him to do extra work, Samory explained, since he understood about Samory's lack of background in the subject.

Samory stated that to deal with the problem of multiple choice questions, he needed to study more so that he was "more familiar with the information that the questions cover." He stated that these tests would continue to be hard for him because he didn't have the test-taking background necessary to do well on multiple choice questions. However, he felt that if he studied hard, he could minimize this lack of background. He felt that the more of these types of tests that he took, the more he would feel comfortable with them. He found, for example, that when he practiced for the TOEFL test, he got more comfortable with the style of the test, and therefore did better on it. Samory emphasized that he had "no critique of the teacher or the test style." Rather, he felt that it was his own job to get used to the testing style. Overall, however, he reasserted that the main problem was the lack of background knowledge in the subject.

Samory also experienced some problems while getting started on his project. He stated that he was not able to understand how to begin the project, so he asked his classmate for help on getting started. She was willing to help and gave him some advice on how to get started. After that, he stated, he was able to do things on his own. He stated that this was often the case – he didn't know where to begin, but once he started, everything went along well. Therefore, he had found it very effective to ask for help from his friends in the early stages of a project. He reported that his classmates and friends were very willing to help. Once again, however, he blamed his problems in this class on his lack of background knowledge.

At this point in the semester, Samory maintained that his goal was simply to get through the class. He didn't want to worry too much about it, since he only wanted to get some general ideas about soil management and wouldn't be working directly in the field. His strategy currently was to do some extra credit work and also to put more energy into memorizing the data. He stated that the final exam in this class would contain one hundred comprehensive multiple choice questions. However, the instructor had given them a list of one hundred points that they needed to know, so he felt that it should be enough to memorize this data set to pass that part of the test. Samory expressed confidence about the test, as long as he was able to memorize the list.

As observed in the classroom, the instructor had given the students an outline of notes in a packet, so everyone was able to follow along directly with the lectures. Students needed only to add extra notes to this outline. Samory stated that he had added extra information as the lecture proceeded. He found that with this style, it was easy to follow along with the lecture. He felt that the extra notes he added covered everything that he needed to know. He felt that it would be hard to follow the lectures without these notes. But note taking was not difficult for him in this class, he claimed. He stated that, overall, he had not experienced too many problems taking notes this semester; since his other instructors followed along with the book and put notes on the blackboard, lectures were easy for him to follow.

Samory felt that it was difficult to study in a foreign language, but that it was particularly difficult to study in a foreign language in a class where you had no background knowledge. He felt more confident about the upcoming semester, since he would be taking classes where he had a stronger background. His plan at that point was to start to learn things ahead of time and to start reading ahead of time, which he had not done this semester. He also stated that he needed to put more effort into reading and studying early in the semester. He felt that if he had read the book before the semester began, giving some of the words and concepts some time to sink in, he would have had an easier time. Instead, he felt that he had spent the semester just trying to catch up to where the instructor was.

For the remainder of the semester, Samory claimed that he was trying to multiply his efforts. He knew that he only had a short time left in the semester, so he felt that he had to put more energy into memorization. At the beginning of the semester, he thought that he could "just read the book and understand." Now, however, he realized that he had to put more effort into it, especially early in the semester.

Samory stated that he was an "average student" back in his home country, but that he didn't want to be an average student here. Therefore, his plan was "to get no sleep for the next few weeks," to "do extra work, whatever it takes," and to "work hard!" He stated that he always got nine or ten points out of ten possible points on all of his homework. Homework was no problem, he felt, as long as he had time to think about it. It was just the pressure and lack of time when taking a multiple choice test that created problems for him.

The Final Interview

The final interview for Samory took place just after the end of the spring semester. Samory stated that, in the end, the Soil Resources class turned out "O.K." After the previous interview, he wrote the extra credit paper that he had discussed and got a "very good grade on it, an A." He stated that he had no problems with doing written work. Give him a topic and enough time, he claimed, and everything was fine. He got a very bad grade on his final exam, however. Because he did well on all the homework and the take home papers, though, he got a passing grade, which was his main goal.

Samory stated that the style of the final examination was still a problem for him. He said that a fellow student from his home country also had the same problem. First, he stated, he didn't like multiple choice exams and simply had no background in them. Second, he had "lost the habit of doing exercises and tests in class." While he took tests in the IEP, they were not the same type or style of test. Any tests that he took in his undergraduate days were of a different style. In his undergraduate program, students were given a topic, then plenty of time to answer the question, so there really wasn't much pressure. Therefore, he had no experience dealing with taking tests under pressure.

Samory felt that if he had been given a different type of test, he would have done fine. Once again, the final test for Soil Resources was divided up into three parts. The first section, the multiple choice section, consisted of forty questions. The second part asked him to answer two essay questions. The third part was on math problems. Once again, he did well on the essay and math sections, but poorly on the multiple choice section. Because there were so many multiple choice questions, his grade was reduced considerably.

Samory stated that he felt that the IEP could have helped him more to practice multiple choice tests. He felt that it would have been a good idea to teach different skills such as different testing styles. He felt that the IEP reading and grammar classes would have been a good place for that.

Samory also had some problems with multiple choice questions on the tests for his Environmental Economics course. He stated that he only got seventy five percent on the first exam, due largely to his poor performance on multiple choice questions. However, he did receive an eighty two percent on the second test. Thus, he did feel that his test taking ability had improved with practice and that since he had gained some experience with them, he felt that he would do better on such tests in the future. He reiterated, however, that he wished he had had some practice while still in the IEP.

Samory was quick to point out that he had to take some of the responsibility for the problem. He stated that he "can't change the situation or expect the teacher to change his style" just for him. He reasserted that he felt that if he didn't have the vocabulary or background knowledge from the area, multiple choice questions were difficult for him to answer. Therefore, he stated that he believed it was a lack of vocabulary and background knowledge, combined with an unfamiliarity with the testing style, that had caused his greatest problems. It was, he stated, a combination of "both study and practice" that would help him in the future.

Samory related, as an example, a story about his time in the intensive English program in the other university that he attended. When he first arrived there, he took a test and was placed at the lowest level offered. After going to one class, however, he was immediately advanced up. He felt that the problem was that his ability on tests didn't reflect his true state of knowledge or language learning ability, or any ability for that matter. Samory stated that when a test got closer, he got more and more anxious.

Samory stated that he did fine in writing, however. He had some experience writing for his former jobs, plus learned from his friends on the job how to write "in the American style." His paper for the Computer Applications class "looked pretty good" and was evaluated well, so he expected a good grade on it. He had trouble with the class project, however, because "the data was bad." He was not able to overlay one year over the other to determine land use changes. Because this was not his fault, however, the instructor was understanding. The instructor asked him to just write the paper and hand it in as it was. He stated that he had learned quite a bit about the computer software program, knowledge that he would be able to use in the future.

In addition, he got the highest score in the class for the final paper in his Environmental Economics class. In that paper, he discussed the situation in his home country, a subject that he knew a great deal about, so he therefore received a good grade. This had reinforced Samory's belief that the more familiar with a subject he was, the better grade he would receive. And the more experience he had, he added, the better he would do in the future.

His plan for the future was to begin to read ahead for future classes. He planned to use the time between the spring and summer semesters to spend some time reading books for the classes that he would be taking. He stated that he also planned to use the time between the summer and fall semesters to read ahead for the fall semester.

Samory also planned to meet with some professors to see if it was possible to audit their courses in the fall. He wanted to just "go and listen to the lectures" to "learn things in a relaxed way." In this way, he hoped to get some help in learning the specialized vocabulary that he felt he needed to know.

Mari

"Everything takes time!"

The Background Interview

At the time of the study, Mari was a twenty year old female undergraduate from Asia. She was majoring in English and was on a one-year exchange program from a university in her home country at the time of the study. Her first and only language of the home was an Asian language and her parents spoke only that language. In addition to studying English, she also took courses in one other Asian language during her freshman and sophomore years of college.

Mari stated that she felt that language learning was "necessary." Her first experiences with English came from watching English movies with her parents when she was young. Her formal learning of English, however, began in junior high school and continued "for the next eight or nine years through college." These classes, she stated, were "very tiring." She reported that this study was almost exclusively grammatical in nature. She was happy while in high school that her English courses were relatively easy, but wished, by the time of the study, that they had been harder and that she had put more effort into her studies.

In senior high school, she had a native English speaking teacher for conversation class. In addition, she also took English classes at a preparatory school "almost every day" and "on vacations and in the summer." She also had the experience of a ten day home-stay in the United States while in high school. It was in high school that she decided to become an English major.

Mari's main reason for studying English was that "you can use English anywhere in the world." As an English major, however, she felt that English was not so useful in daily life in her home country. She felt that she couldn't practice language communicatively in her home country. Her incentive to learn English at the time of the study was that she had to take an English test after college. If she did well on the test, it would greatly improve her chances of getting a better job.

She stated that the problem in learning English in her home country was that teachers there only "teach what they know," which in her opinion was primarily grammatical in nature and not communicative in nature.

Mari came to The University in May of 1998, when she began taking classes in the IEP. She stated that she was studying in America to improve her English, which would help her find a better job. She wanted to find a job in which she could use English; therefore, whether or not she could use English would be a deciding factor in her future job choice.

She stated that she enjoyed studying English and other languages "because it can help me communicate with people and can understand their cultures." She saw English as a tool for global communication. With English, she felt, she could go anywhere in the world and communicate with people. She also enjoyed writing in that she could put down her opinions on paper.

Mari stated that her parents were initially less than enthusiastic about her coming to America, as they thought it was not a safe place to live. When she made them aware of her "strong opinion" about studying there, however, they began to support her decision.

Her short term goals included "learning English as much as possible" in the relatively short time that she was in America. She wanted to learn to be "fluent and natural and smooth." She stated that she wanted to be a person "who can explain or express her opinion." She said that in the future she wanted people to have a deeper understanding of what she said or believed. She also wanted to make many friends, not only Americans, but international friends as well.

Mari believed that there were two kinds of people at The University. The first were people "like the IEP teachers" who had experience learning languages or living in other countries. These people tried to understand what non-native speakers of English said, she felt. They "have an ear to listen to international students," even if those students use the wrong grammar or wrong verb. On the other hand, there are those who "don't understand anything I say." When she tried to explain something to them, they said they couldn't understand, she reported. She believed that "they don't want to understand and they are closed-minded."

In the long-term, Mari wanted to change stereotypes that people had of each other, for example stereotypes that Americans had about people from her home country and vice-versa. To that end, she found herself often trying to explain the culture of her home country to her friends in the United States. She stated that she wanted to find American friends when she returned home, and hoped to someday study in America further.

She stated that her ideas about America before arrival were that America was a big place with friendly, out-going people, but that it was a dangerous place. She stated that she chose The University because there were few people from her home country studying there, so that she wouldn't end up speaking her own language all the time. Her image of American college life was that if you didn't study hard, you would fail, unlike a college in her home country, where you could study "right before the test and still pass." Therefore, she thought that every student attended every class and studied hard. She stated that she was quite surprised to find out that this wasn't true of American college students.

Mari believed that she understood American culture "pretty well" and had adapted to life in America fairly well. It had caused her "to change her mind" in that she had become stronger mentally, she claimed, because "you need to have a strong opinion to live here." However, she admitted that it was still not easy for her to freely express her opinions. She believed that overall she did not experience culture shock when first coming to America, mainly due to her previous home-stay experience. She did feel, however, that in certain situations, she still experienced some culture shock, but for the most part these smaller episodes were going away.

Mari was surprised, however, by the way that students acted in class, for example by putting their feet on chairs in the classroom, which would be considered highly disrespectful in a classroom in her home country. She was also surprised at how students asked questions so openly in class, as opposed to students in her home country who generally waited until after class to ask the instructor questions.

Mari stated that she occasionally read the student newspaper; otherwise, the only reading she did in English was for class. When she first came to The University, she tried to write letters and email in English, but now she had no time, she reported. She stated that it took too much time to write letters. She did, however, speak English every day, though she still had trouble speaking in class. She especially enjoyed teaching people about the culture of her home country.

She worried "a little bit" about reading in the future, because she knew that she "will have to read a lot." The vocabulary in certain areas also frustrated her. Writing, on the other hand, didn't worry her too much because she said that it came easy and she could "use my own words." Listening worried her a little also, but not as much as speaking, which caused her the most worry. This, she felt, was her biggest problem, although it depended on who she was talking to, she reported. Mari felt that she lacked confidence and was afraid of being embarrassed in class and was "afraid of people not understanding" her.

She perceived her ability to read as being strong, as long as she was interested in the subject. If so, then she could read quite fast. If the subject matter was boring, however, she read slowly. She felt that she still had a "limited vocabulary," but she did try to guess meaning from context. She reported that if she couldn't guess, then she would use a dictionary. Speaking in a normal conversation didn't present her with much difficulty, she claimed. Speaking in class, however, caused her the most problems, especially in a course with specialized vocabulary. Listening was also easy, she stated, if she had a high interest in the subject.

She perceived her ability to learn languages as "not so high or natural." As far as library skills went, she felt that she didn't have too much experience, which she felt could hold her back. She stated that her note taking ability depended on the class; specialized vocabulary really got in her way, she related. She also felt that she was not good at questioning and was generally afraid to ask questions in class. She stated, however, that she tried to think "in a positive way," since she felt that attitude was very important in language learning.

The Second Interview

The second interview with Mari was conducted approximately three weeks into the spring semester. During that semester, Mari was taking seven different classes and was therefore very busy. She was taking two business courses, Business Correspondence and Microcomputers, one Volleyball class, one English Composition class, one History of Western Civilization class, one foreign language class, and one Choir class. She stated that she was taking the classes that she wanted to take, that the classes were all her choice. However, she now felt that she was "much too busy."

The Volleyball course that she was taking had turned out not to be what she expected it to be. She expected it to be a routine physical education course, in which she would simply play volleyball every day. However, the class had actually turned out to be a course for physical education majors in which they learned how to teach others to play volleyball. Therefore, she had to do research for the course, learn the history and rules of the sport, and "understand the connection between volleyball and persons who had disabilities." She felt at this point that it was all good information to know and was very interesting, but was somewhat useless since she would never be a physical education teacher and that "the class is a lot of work for only two credits."

She did like the style of the teacher, though. She stated that he "is good and explains how to teach." She was not sure if the vocabulary would offer her any trouble or not at that point. She stated that she had taken volleyball courses in her home country in the past and thus knew the terminology of the sport in her native language, but not in English. In addition, she asserted that she was somewhat worried about the research required for the course.

Mari described her Business Correspondence course as "learning how to write business letters and how to communicate in business." She stated that thus far she had learned only the basics. The class took place in a regular classroom, with work done on computers outside of class on the students' own time. She stated that the teacher was "very nice, very helpful."

Mari's Microcomputers class was a three hour, once-a-week class. Mari stated that she liked that style of course because she could concentrate on the subject better. She stated that the standard fifty minutes was not enough for her to get into a subject. However, the class, in which students sat and worked at computers for the entire period, was tiring.

She stated that she felt the most comfortable in this class, however, for two reasons. The first was that this class was partly a review of what she had learned in a previous computer course in her home country, which made it easier for her "to understand the lectures." However, once again, while she was familiar with the concepts, she learned the terms in her native language, not English. The second reason for feeling comfortable in the class was that, because the students are all seated at computers, the teacher was able to come around to each of them individually at their computer terminals. This had made it much easier for Mari to ask questions of the instructor when she didn't understand something.

Mari stated that she was taking the foreign language course primarily as a way to practice her speaking and listening abilities. She didn't feel that she could put too much effort into this class, however, because "English was first." She didn't want her study of the foreign language to get in the way of her learning of English. She stated that she only wanted "small conversation." Speaking, she said, was tough for her, though. She just didn't dare to put too much effort into it. She felt that if she were in a different situation, an environment where she actually had the time to concentrate on learning the language, she would put more effort into it and would make more progress.

In this class, Mari stated that she was highly reluctant to ask a question. She stated that she didn't want to "interrupt the flow" of the class. She felt that she had no confidence in asking questions in English. She felt that asking a question would require more time for the instructor to answer for her than for the others in the class, who were all native speakers of English. If she had trouble, she stated, she would ask the instructor questions after the class, in much the same way that she would do in her home country. She claimed that she felt very comfortable going up to the teacher after class and asking questions. She stated that she now found the sounds of the other language she was studying "strange," and the sounds of English "more normal."

Mari stated that the English Composition class was the one that kept her the busiest. She stated that she liked writing, but that for this class she had to write "five journal entries per week," in addition to five larger essays; therefore, this class alone took up a significant amount of her time. "The class," she stated, "is very time consuming."

Mari stated that of all her classes, the English Composition class was where she did the most talking, primarily because the students were expected to get into groups and discuss the class material. She stated that she would "rather just sit back and take notes," but that this was impossible. She didn't feel comfortable explaining her opinions and she feared that her speech was "not natural." She was also worried that the instructor would focus on her grammar, which she didn't feel terribly confident about.

Mari reported two surprising aspects of this class. The first was that she was surprised that students would so openly complain about the number of journal entries required in the class. And even more, she was surprised by the instructor's reaction, which was telling the student, "If you don't like it, drop the class." She felt that such teacher-student exchanges in her home country would never be "so emotional" and would be of a "much more indirect style."

A second occurrence that she found strange was that the instructor misspelled words when writing them on the blackboard. Mari found this highly unusual, since her conception of an English teacher was someone who knew how to spell very well. She felt that an English teacher "really ought to know how to spell," since her writing on the blackboard could serve to confuse Mari. For example, when she tried to find a misspelled word in the dictionary, she couldn't find it. This forced her to search through the dictionary for other possible spellings, but she stated that this strategy was not very successful. She said that she expected the word to be spelled right and when it was not, she felt that she "can't learn the word."

The History of Western Civilization class was also keeping her busy, since she had to read a great deal. For this class, she had to read two novels and a book of poems, all of which she had to read and then write essays over, as well as having to read "a big textbook." While she enjoyed reading, it all took a lot of time. "Everything takes time!," she exclaimed. She stated that she found it easier to read the textbook than the novels, though she was surprised to see the size of American textbooks. Textbooks in her home country, she explained, were much smaller.

Mari stated that this class was the biggest class that she had ever been a part of. Because of the large class size, "only a few people ask questions," while most do not. She stated that she would "never" dare ask a question in a class that was this size. It would be too intimidating, she related. Therefore, she simply did her best to understand the lecture. She also attended review sessions, which were conducted by the class's two assistants. She stated that she felt much more comfortable going to the review sessions to ask questions, since the group size was so much smaller.

The Choir class was the class that took up the least amount of her time, she reported. For this course, Mari only had to attend classes and perform at two concerts to receive credit. There were no tests or quizzes, she remarked, "you just have to show up." The teacher was also "funny and enjoyable," which made the class an easy one to attend.

Mari stated that in all of the classes that she was taking, notes could be hard to take. Her present strategy was to first write down all of the words that she didn't understand. She would then check her textbooks after class for the terms, since most terms "are coming from the book." If she couldn't find the term in the book or the dictionary, or figure it out on her own, her next step was to ask one of her former IEP instructors for help. She stated that she didn't want to interrupt any of her classes to ask about a term, since she believed that everyone in the class would know the term and she would be embarrassed. Additionally, once again, she was concerned about interrupting the flow of the class.

The Third Interview

The third interview with Mari was delayed somewhat, as she had been busy completing her midterms. She reported that she was still taking all seven classes, which had kept her very busy. She stated that she was "so happy" to be finished with her tests. She stated that her midterms "went O.K.," but she was not very confident about her History of Western Civilization class midterm exam.

In the History class, she claimed that she had "too much to read and too much to do." She stated, however, that the professor "is really, really nice" and gave her the benefit of the doubt. She stated that she always attended the study sessions that were offered, but she still couldn't understand everything. She felt that there were "lots of new words." She stated that even though she studied history in her country, she couldn't understand "because it is in English."

Because of all the new words, she asked the instructor for a copy of his notes. She initially hesitated to ask for the notes, but found that he was "really helpful." The instructor was very nice to her and told her, "Next time, don't hesitate to ask for notes." She stated that she was surprised because she "did not expect that kind of an answer."

The notes, however, were still not enough, she asserted. The notes were "a lot, all hand writing, really hard to read." They took too much time to decipher, she stated, and didn't give all the details and information she needed. Therefore, the instructor suggested that she ask one of the graduate assistants for a set of notes, because they usually wrote notes while in class. Mari felt that this instructor was so helpful to her because he had studied Spanish in a foreign country previously and had therefore had similar experiences with hers, so he understood the problems Mari was experiencing.

Mari reported that she found the study sessions to be useful. She found that the students asked a lot more questions during the study sessions. The study sessions, she stated, "tell what the main points are." In conjunction with the class quizzes, she felt that this told her what would be on the following test.

She also stated that she had difficulty keeping up with the readings. There was simply not enough time, she felt, to complete them all. Time, she stated, was her biggest problem overall. In addition to the reading for this class, she also had a tremendous amount of reading in her other classes, with much new vocabulary to learn in all of her classes. She had started reading one of the required novels, she reported, which she found "much more difficult than reading a textbook." Textbooks, she stated, "explain what happens and give definitions. Novel doesn't do that." She stated that she planned to give up on reading the novels because they were too difficult. Even if she looked words up in the dictionary, she explained, she couldn't understand the novel, unlike a textbook.

For this class, she reported that she had to take a lot of notes. Sometimes, she stated, even if she heard the word but didn't recognize it, she had a hard time writing it down. She tried to look these words up in a dictionary, but because she was writing down the spelling from hearing the word, she couldn't always find it.

She felt that this was where the instructor's notes would be most useful. She stated that she only slept for four hours a night during midterms. To keep herself awake while studying, she switched back and forth between subjects.

At this point she had learned all the Volleyball class "moves." The next step for the class was to show that she could teach the techniques by teaching the other students in the class. Then she would be required to modify the game to make it accessible to disabled persons. She stated, however, that she had a hard time explaining things in English. She claimed that she especially had a hard time explaining things in English when she was nervous or in a tense situation such as teaching. She stated that the others in the class were nice and patient with her, but she could tell from their faces that things were less than perfect when she was demonstration teaching.

Mari had started to do some of the research required for the class, which was due after spring break. She stated that she didn't like using the library's computer system to find sources. The process, she said, took too long. She felt that she had the skills necessary, but it was just too difficult to find the right kind of materials, given the large amount of materials in the library that she had to sort through.

Mari stated that she had played volleyball for a long time, had the necessary background knowledge, and knew how to "make the moves," but she just didn't have the English vocabulary for explaining it to others. She felt that she had "to learn to use the English terms." She stated that she knew the terms in her native language, but didn't know how to explain the moves in English. She felt that she needed more time memorizing the English terms and especially the specialized education vocabulary.

Mari described her Business Correspondence class at this point as being "pretty tough." While the instructor was nice, the specialized vocabulary was difficult. She had to write business letters for this class, which required her to imagine different situations. Then she was required to write letters that fit the various situations. She had found that learning the physical parts of a business letter was easy, but writing the body of the letter so that it fit the situation was difficult. She felt that this "is not an English language problem, it is a culture problem." She felt that she did not have the ability to persuade someone in a letter. As part of weekly quizzes for the class, they had to read and understand the meanings of certain business letters. She felt that while she could understand the individual words, she could not understand the meaning behind the large passages. It was hard, she stated, "to express the idea of a letter."

The Microcomputer class, on the other hand, was the "easiest class" because she had had a similar class before. In this class, she had a written test and a performance test. She stated that the written examination was fine, but the performance examination gave her some problems. She studied for the test and knew the functions, but time was limited. She had to first read and understand the directions, then execute the functions. Once again, the material was hard to understand because it was business oriented. Therefore, it wasn't the software functions that gave her a difficult time, but rather understanding the directions, and understanding them quickly enough to complete the functions on time, that caused her the most problems.

The English Composition class was the class that kept her the busiest, Mari reported. In this class, she had to write five journal entries per week. She didn't find this activity difficult, she claimed, just time consuming. Also, to write the essays took a long time, she reported. She had already written three essays at this point in the semester. She had found that the amount of time a journal entry took depended on the topic. Some took longer than others. If she knew something about the topic or was very interested in it, she could finish the entry quickly. If she didn't know anything about the topic, it could take up to an hour. She had found also, however, that if she really knew the topic and liked it, the journal entry became more like an essay than a journal entry, so she ended up spending a lot of time on it. When she wrote, she stated, she felt that she could explain her opinion, since she had time to think about what she wanted to say. Speaking was harder because she didn't "have time to think."

Each time before writing an essay, Mari explained, the students in her writing class had to do some research on a topic. She stated that before writing their own essays they had to read many essays in class, then find extra articles related to those essays in the library. She stated that many of the essays that the class read were abstract, and thus hard to make "connections to my own opinion." Although the instructor took the class to the library at the beginning of the semester, the research was hard because she didn't "know where to start."

Mari had found that the instructor did not correct the grammar in her essays, that she was focusing on the "opinions" expressed in her essays. She had also found that the instructor did not "correct" her journal entries and that she only read them. Once again, this went contrary to Mari's expectations of an English instructor.

Mari stated that she had group work in her English Composition class. For each essay that they had to write, they had to get into small groups in class to "correct essays with other students" and help them revise their papers. In these groups, each student had to read their papers aloud, then the other members of the group made oral comments. Mari stated that this was "really hard because they talk fast." She said that she didn't have such a hard time stating her opinion in the peer groups, but had a hard time understanding when they read their papers. If she could read the paper and take her time, she stated, she didn't have any problem talking about the paper, as long as she had an opinion. She stated that it was easier for her to express her opinions in these small groups, while in big classes, there was "no way" that she would speak up. She reiterated that it worked the same way in study sessions. She would ask a question in the study session, as long as she was confident about asking the question correctly, though she explained that she was usually too busy taking notes to have time to think of questions.

Mari also expressed surprise at seeing how "lazy" her fellow students were in this class. She stated that everyone was supposed to bring an essay to class on the days that they had peer groups, but some students only had one roughly written page, while some students had nothing written at all. She explained that the students would say, "I didn't have enough time." She found this very "irritating" since, in spite of having seven classes and having to spend more time on any given paper than the rest of the students in the class because of the language factor, she always had a paper prepared and they didn't.

Mari also had some group work in Business Correspondence. In these groups, the students worked on coming up with "communication topics and situations" and then discussed these topics. In the groups, the students were told to "work as an employee of a company" and to "work through the situation." They had to decide, as a group, what kind of correspondence they should use to solve the problem or how they would handle the situation. Then one member of the group had to stand up and present the group's consensus. This group, reported Mari, was slightly larger than the writing class group, with seven people, and even this larger number made the group work "a little tougher." She stated that she had a hard time "to keep up with everyone's ideas." She stated that she sometimes had a hard time understanding what they are talking about, especially if she didn't understand the situation that they are talking about. She felt that if she had more time to think about the situation, she could more easily express her opinion. However, all group work was done in the class setting and was thus done under rather rushed circumstances.

Mari stated that she felt that she had accomplished her goals at this point in the semester, although she felt that, in retrospect, she should had done more to keep up with all of her classes, especially at the beginning of the semester. Mari also stated that she was not getting any outside help on any of her schoolwork. She claimed that she had not even asked any of her friends for help.

Mari commented that in her IEP speaking class, the focus was often on "chatting." However, in her Volleyball class, she had to teach or present how to do something. She felt this went for her peer group experiences as well. She didn't just need to know how to chat, she asserted, she needed to know how to present. She wished that she knew more about how to do presentations and speeches, and knew more about the American style of teaching.

She also stated that in her IEP listening class, she felt that she would have benefited from listening to more varied voices. She felt that she would like to have heard real people, not just tapes. She felt that the lectures were simply too easy; the people on the tapes spoke clearly, but people in real life didn't speak that way. There was much more unclear speech in real life, she felt, based on her experiences during this half semester.

At this point in the semester, listening and speaking were of primary concern for Mari, as she could take her time when reading and writing. However, she also stated that she needed to learn to read faster in order to keep up with all of her classes. She stated that it would had been helpful to have learned some of the terminology of her major in her IEP reading class. The Microcomputer class, for example, she stated, had been tough for her, since she had never learned those terms in English before.

The Classroom Observation

The classroom observation for Mari was conducted during her Business Correspondence course. During the classroom observation, Mari sat near the back of the class, near the center of the back wall. This classroom was in rows of fixed chairs, each on an ascending level. There was a dais at the front with a podium. There were approximately twenty five students in the class.

During the course of an hour and a half, the instructor lectured almost continuously, usually in reference to an overhead transparency. During most of the class, Mari sat with her head looking down at the textbook used in the class, except when the instructor made an explicit reference to the overhead being discussed, when Mari would look up briefly. When a new overhead transparency was placed, Mari would look up and take a few notes. Then her head would go back down to looking at the textbook.

On several occasions, Mari took out her bilingual dictionary and looked up words that she had seen on the overhead transparency. She then wrote down the meaning of the word in her notebook.

The instructor for this class occasionally asked the students to answer a question, but did not point to any specific person when doing so. Mari never raised her hand or verbally offered any answers. In fact, when the instructor asked questions, Mari did not raise her head. Only the students who volunteered to answer questions were called on. This was a limited number of students, with the same students answering questions repeatedly. Mari, from the time that she entered the classroom until she left, did not have any verbal contact with anyone.

The Fourth Interview

Mari stated that in the class observed, her Business Correspondence class, vocabulary continued to be a problem, but she felt that this was only part of the problem for her. She stated that she felt that she could understand the meaning of most of the individual words, but not the meaning that the letter as a whole carried. The grammar of her letters was fine, she claimed, but the "intention" behind the letters continued to be a problem. She compared this problem to the distinction that was made in her native language between "casual and formal situations." In her native language, even if one knew the grammar and words to use, it didn't mean that one could conduct themselves properly in a given situation. She felt that the same thing applied in writing business letters. Mari stated that she knew English grammar, but didn't believe that she got the "right feel." While she felt comfortable with English grammar, she didn't feel comfortable with which words to use in different situations. She also had a difficult time deciding what level of formality to use in different types of letters. She stated that she did still have a couple of grammar problems, but not enough to get in the way.

Mari reported that unlike in the class that was observed, the instructor often had them get into groups to discuss situations. It was during these discussions that she really began to see that she did not understand the implications of the letters. While the others in the group freely discussed what type of letter to use and why, Mari had a hard time making any contribution to the discussion because she didn't have "an opinion" on which type of letter to use. She stated that she felt slightly embarrassed that she could not contribute to the discussion.

Mari stated that she didn't really ask anyone for help in this class. None of her friends had taken this class, she reported, so she didn't feel that they would be of any help to her. She reiterated that she would feel very uncomfortable stopping the instructor's lecture to ask a question. Therefore, she preferred to ask the teacher questions after class. She stated that the instructor was "really nice and could understand my situation and was very helpful," but that "it was still hard."

When asked to explain further, Mari admitted that she usually just asked simple questions of the instructor after class, often grammatical questions, because she felt that the instructor "was too busy" to deal with her problems. She preferred instead "to just go home and study more." She stated that with this strategy, the class had gone "all right."

The Final Interview

The final interview with Mari took place just before she was about to return to her home country. She had taken some of her final examinations early so that she could return home as soon as possible. At the time of the interview, she had finished all five of the final exams that she needed to take. She didn't have any exams in her Choir or English Composition classes.

Mari stated that in the Business Correspondence course, the test was "tough, but all right." Even up to the end of the semester, she reported, language was a problem. She reiterated that she didn't have a problem with grammar. Her problem was writing letters that would actually have the thrust that they were intended to have. She once again cited the problem of formality. She expanded, explaining that she also worried about being polite in letters, while still being strong enough to get her point across.

The Microcomputers class, Mari stated simply, was "kind of a review" for her. She stated that by taking the class, she could "learn again," something that she found very helpful to get the knowledge "into my head." She found the vocabulary for this class much easier, since much of it was a review for her.

Her foreign language class also went well, she reported. She stated that she didn't want to put too much time into that class. She said that she was "learning [the other language] by English, just in the classroom," which she didn't believe worked too well. There was too much English in the class and not enough of the foreign language, she believed. She stated that sometimes when the teacher explained grammar points, the terms she used were very difficult for her to understand. This did not bother her very much, however, since she was only taking the class "for fun." Mari stated that in this class, she was comfortable with reading and writing, but not speaking. She felt that if she had the opportunity to concentrate on the other language, it would be much easier, but with so many classes, she just didn't have time. She stated that she felt her other classes were more important for her to concentrate on.

In her English class, she stated, she could not finish all of her journal entries on time. She had to write six essays for the class, she reported. When she could concentrate on writing essays, she stated, the writing went well. She could revise them and work with a tutor. This style, she felt, could help her with her English. She felt that the journal entries could have been helpful, but only if she had had enough time "to do them right." However, with no time to concentrate on them because of her heavy course load, they simply became busy work. In the end, with seven classes to worry about, she was not able to finish all the journal entries on time and simply turned in her journal incomplete.

Mari reported that she had just finished the final exam for her History of Western Civilization class prior to the interview. She was taking this class for transfer credit to her home university; therefore, she felt she needed to put more effort into that class than some of the other classes. The hardest aspect of the class, according to Mari, was the terminology. This required a great deal of memory work, she reported. She stated that she had taken history courses before, but in her native language. She said that she initially thought that she knew what she would need to know to pass the class, only in her native language, and at first thought that she would only have to transfer the words from one language to the other. However, she reported that she now thinks differently. The problem, as she saw it, was the style of the teacher, which was very different from the style of history teachers in her home country. There, she stated, she was expected to know names and dates. Therefore, in her home country, she could just study on her own and memorize the names and dates. At The University, she stated, the teacher expected his or her students to understand and "interpret" history, which she felt made the class much harder than she expected. Therefore, the experiences in her home country and in America didn't match up, making the class a difficult one for her.

A further problem, according to Mari, was that she could never get all of the information she needed to know through listening to lectures. She tried to take notes; however, the instructor didn't write too much on the board, as the instructors in her home country would had done, once again causing a mismatch. Instead, the instructor would write down the person's name or write down an issue on the board, then talk about that person or issue. When the instructor would begin to talk about the person or issue, she stated that she couldn't catch everything that the instructor said. It was just too much information for her to process at one time. She stated that the specialized terms and names were hard to get the first time without having seen it in writing previously. She stated that names are especially difficult.

Because of the large amount of reading for this class, Mari reported that she didn't try to read everything. Instead, she stated, she just scanned the readings. She tried to read her notes and understand and interpret. She also reported giving up on reading the novels, since there wasn't enough time. She stated that the class was not what she expected. She had wanted to learn more about American history, since she was an English major, but that the class did not turn out to be about that subject. She would rather have taken an American history course, she reported.

In her Volleyball class, she reported, she enjoyed the volleyball playing aspect, but found that the other work that she had to do for this course was much more that she had expected. At the end of the semester, she had to turn in a fourteen page paper. She stated that she had never written a fourteen page paper in her life, not even in her native language. However, she proudly exclaimed, "I did it!", and felt that she "did O.K.," so she was content. She stated that the vocabulary in this class was no problem at the end because it was a direct transfer from vocabulary that she already knew in her first language. She stated that she found transferring the direct word from her native language to English much easier. At least, she reported, it was easier than in the history class, because the philosophical basis for the class had been so different from what she had come to expect of a history class in her home country.

Mari stated that her Choir class "was just fun." She stated that it was fun to sing in English. She felt that this class was good pronunciation practice, since they did pronunciation/enunciation drills and practiced reading the words out loud before singing a song. She believed that it helped her overall pronunciation. She felt that it would be a good class for other IEP students to take since it was a way to practice pronunciation while having fun and making friends at the same time.

She felt that she could now understand the words in music much better. She stated that she still couldn't catch every word, but felt that her listening skills had gotten much better.

Mari reported that her main goal at present was to return to The University in the future to study and hoped to apply for a scholarship so that she could return. However, she still had one year remaining in her program back in her home country. In the meantime, she stated that she planned to keep studying English. She was afraid, however, that her English level would begin to decline. She stated that to try to avoid this, she would try to write to her friends here in the United States on the internet, to watch CNN and other news programs, and to listen to English radio and music. She also planned to buy books and magazines to bring back with her to her home country. Her goal was to at least keep her present level of English, and if possible, to raise her level higher. She stated that some of her American friends would be going to her country on an exchange program, so she hoped to be able to see them there and have the chance to converse in English. Other people in her home country who spoke English would be hard to find, however.

Mari stated that she had found a big difference between the writing that she did for her IEP writing classes and the writing she had to do for her mainstream English Composition course. She stated that it was hard to make the adjustment between them. She stated that she "learned a lot of writing rules" that she didn't learn in her IEP classes. She felt that this was a good course to take, but having more of a transition would had been more helpful. She felt that the "connection between the classes" should be made "smoother."

She also stated that there was a big difference between speaking in an IEP speaking class and speaking in mainstream classes. In the IEP speaking classes, she said, "classes are small and everybody knows each other." Therefore, she felt that everyone could do a good job of speaking in these classes. In mainstream classes, however, there were too many people that didn't know each other. In her

IEP classes, there were only international students, she stated, and everyone got to know each other well. In mainstream classes, however, students "treat each other like strangers." She stated that she feared speaking or presenting in front of Americans for this reason. The more presentations she gave, she claimed, the worse she felt. She hated to see the uncomfortable looks on her classmates' faces. She stated that there was therefore the need to present not just in front of IEP classmates, but in front of others as well. She felt that it would be best to practice in front of classmates first. Then, she felt, "all the speaking classes could get together to practice." Then, they "could present in front of other classes" in the IEP. Finally, they "could practice presenting in front of [IEP] instructors."

In IEP listening classes, she felt that "students need to hear lots of different voices." They need unclear speech, she stated. She stated that there was a big difference between the lectures that students listened to on tape in her IEP classes and the lectures that she heard in mainstream classes. She also felt that the solution to this would be similar to the process she suggested for listening, once again done in steps.

In reading courses, she stated, with practice she had gotten better. She also stated that she felt students needed to learn to be more efficient, not just faster, and needed to learn "what to read and what not to read."

Romulo

"I like to find three or four ways to go."

The Background Interview

At the time of the study, Romulo was a twenty-seven year old male undergraduate from South America majoring in public relations. Although he was an undergraduate at The University, he did have a bachelor's degree in advertising from a university in his home country.

His first language was a Romance language and both his mother and father were monolingual speakers of that language, so it was the language of his home. However, he stated that he did occasionally speak English at home with his sister and brother-in-law, both of whom had lived and studied in an American university and who didn't "want to lose their language." He also reported that his father had spent some time in the United States when he attended an American high school in Connecticut, although Romulo stated that he didn't speak English to his father.

Romulo's wife, who was also a native of his home country, was also studying at The University and thus spoke English. He reported that he spoke English with his wife whenever they were outside of their home, because "we do not want people to think we are talking about them. We want to be polite." They continued to speak their first language in the home, however.

Romulo first began to learn English at six years of age, when he started school in a bilingual elementary school. He attended this school for three years. He reported that half of his classes were in English, the other half in his first language. He stated, however, that he didn't retain any of the English that he learned during this time. He reported that he did not study English again until high school, but this period was characterized by the study of grammar, which he found highly boring. He continued to study English in college, he reported, but that was primarily in the form of study of the specialized vocabulary of advertising. He claimed that in that class the students never practiced speaking in English. He reported that during this period he never had a native speaker of English as a teacher, but he did read some English language books and watched many American movies through an English language cable channel that he watched frequently. At that time, he tried to concentrate on pronunciation, tried to translate what he heard, and tried "to catch as much as possible."

Romulo remarked that the students in his home country usually cared more about English than they did about their college study, since knowing

English could help them get a better job. Therefore, he reported, there were many specialized language centers in his home country. These centers were expensive, however, and were therefore only for the rich or for those families who were willing to sacrifice a great deal to send a family member there.

Romulo had also had the experience of traveling to London previously, as well as coming to America to attend his sister's graduation ceremony from college. During this trip, he and his family traveled throughout the east coast of the United States and Canada. It was at this point that he made the decision to attend college in America. He stated that in his home country, the entire college was housed in one building, so he was highly impressed with the large buildings, the facilities, the number of books in the libraries, and the large number of computers on the campus of the college that his sister attended.

Romulo stated that his father initially didn't want him to come to the United States to study, since he wanted his son to take over the family business. However, he had eventually become supportive of his son's decision. He also stated that his sister and brother-in-law were highly supportive, as was his mother. His mother believed that the bad economy and political situation in his country were good reasons for coming to America. He reported that his mother and sister saw studying in America as a great opportunity.

Romulo claimed that he "didn't really begin to learn English" until he was twenty-four years old, when he first came to study in the United States. When he first arrived in America, he studied at a language academy affiliated with a private university in a large Midwestern city. He arrived there in August 1997 and studied there for one school year, taking virtually all of the courses that the academy offered. He considered this experience a very good one. Because the academy was affiliated with a university, he had the opportunity to live in a dormitory where he had an American roommate, with whom he traded lessons in his native language lessons for English lessons. In addition, he had also held a series of jobs at which he had had "some chances to speak English" and to "learn the names of products and things like that."

Romulo reported that his main reason for learning English was to help himself get a better job, especially with the globalization of English. He felt that reading ability would be important for this. He also commented on how his situation had become inverted over the last year. In his home country, knowing English would help him find a better job; here in America, however, he felt that knowing his native language would help him find a better job.

Romulo's short-term goals included improving his pronunciation, which he hoped to "improve a lot." He reported that he tried to speak English every day, especially with his wife. He stated that they "correct each other all the time." He felt that his wife, though she was not a native speaker, "knows things that I do not and vice-versa." He also stated that he loved to watch television and listen to the radio, and loved to talk and read in English. He also tried to spend some of his working hours talking to coworkers. He believed that it was more important to speak well than to write well, since he had found that "no one here, including native speakers," knew how to write well; therefore, writing did not worry him.

In the long-term, his goal was to find a job with a good company. Romulo stated that he felt that the best way to learn English was to get a good job and learn the language there. He felt that this was the way to learn "professional language." He felt that since he was planning to remain in America, he "needs to know what people here say."

One problem that he had experienced was that since he studied advertising in his home country, the vocabulary of his major actually presented him with some difficulty. He had found that in English they used many of the same words, but these words were often used in slightly, and sometimes significantly, different ways. He stated that in the U.S. the terminology was more consistent between companies than it was in his home country. He stated that learning the vocabulary of his major was hard because he had already learned one way to use this vocabulary and that now he had to learn a different way to use it.

Romulo stated that he felt that he did experience culture shock when first coming to the United States, but only for perhaps the first two weeks. He reported feeling "a little bit lost" during this time. However, soon after arriving in the United States, he met four other people from his home country who helped him adapt to American life greatly.

When first coming to the United States, he thought that it would be easy to make friends here, but found instead that people in America were "closed-minded." In his home country, his classmates would naturally become his friends, but he had not experienced that here. People here, he felt, were "too busy and too competitive" to make friends.

Romulo stated that he did some extra out-of-class reading and liked to read modern novels. He also liked to read books on topics like public presentations and how to talk in public. He also did some extra writing in English, such as writing email messages to his friends and family back home. He called the television "my second wife." He reported that he loved to watch the Discovery Channel and late night talk shows. He reported that thus far, however, he had not had a great deal of interaction with native speakers of English.

Romulo stated that he was somewhat worried about academic writing, which "can be too difficult to understand." He found that the language was often too technical for him. Writing, on the other hand, did not worry him because he had found that others, including native speakers, made mistakes too. He felt that he actually knew more than many native speakers, since he had explicitly studied writing and grammar, which many of them had not. He reported that he was worried about speaking in class at the beginning, but the instructors that he had had in America had encouraged him to voice his opinions, and that he was pushed by his teachers, so that he now felt quite confident to speak. Listening in class did not worry him at all, he reported.

Overall, Romulo rated writing as his weakest skill, followed by speaking, with reading and listening being equal. He felt that he had "fifty percent of the vocabulary I need." He felt that he had the basics down and that reading had helped a great deal with this. He felt that what he needed now was the specialized vocabulary of his major. Other than that, he felt that he could speak naturally.

Romulo stated that he felt that he was a good language learner and liked to learn languages. He didn't like research, however, so he usually took "the easy way out" and depended "too much on shortcuts." He reported that note taking was difficult for him; if he concentrated too much on the notes, he got lost. He claimed that he was more of a visual learner and could remember things much better if the instructor put information on the board than if he only heard the information. He felt that his questioning ability was not very good and that he usually "messes up the verb." He did feel that he had good critical thinking skills, however. He stated that he usually found "three or four ways to go," then talked to people to see "which way is the best."

The Second Interview

When Romulo was interviewed three weeks into the semester, he had begun taking four classes. He was taking two of the classes to satisfy the general study requirements for undergraduates: Astronomy and History of Western Civilization. The other two classes were core classes for his major: Introduction to Public Relations and Communication Graphics.

His Astronomy class counted as part of the general requirements courses that he had to take as an undergraduate. This was a large class, he reported, with "at least seventy five people." He stated that because of the large size of the class, if he sat in the back, he didn't feel like paying attention; therefore, he tried to go to the front of the class and "forget about the rest of the people" in the classroom. He stated that "this is the only way to hear the professor and know what he is talking about."

Overall, Romulo found this course quite easy. He felt familiar with the subject from watching related shows on television. A quiz was given each week in this class, based on the readings that the students had been assigned to do outside of class. Thus far, he stated, he had had no difficulty with the quizzes.

Romulo stated that the instructor for this class was very accessible and easy to talk to. He had already talked to the instructor two times. He said that the instructor was very helpful and even sent him email messages regarding questions that Romulo had asked. He stated that the instructor was "very shy" at the beginning of the semester, but now made jokes with the class to make them more comfortable. He felt that the vocabulary for this class was no problem, since the words were "global words," words that "people around the world use basically the same way."

The Introduction to Western Civilization course that Romulo was taking was an even larger class than the Astronomy course, with "over one hundred and twenty students." Romulo reported that this course was filled with "Latin words and dates." The instructor for this course made an outline that was put on an overhead at the beginning of each class, he reported, which allowed him to know the topic beforehand. He stated that he always wrote the outline down in his notebook, which then allowed him to know and remember which topics to study.

He reported that "the instructor also tries to teach students how to take notes." She would skip one section of the outline on purpose, thereby testing whether students were paying attention or not. The students had to point out the discrepancy to her and point out what part or parts of the outline she had skipped. Romulo stated that he enjoyed this aspect of the class. He felt that since this was a prerequisite course, "it should teach you how to learn." He felt that the instructor really enjoyed what she was doing and was passionate about her subject, which he claimed highly influenced his desire to study well.

Romulo reported that he had a great deal of reading to complete for this course. He had to read five books in total. In addition to the textbook, they had to read four books, including historical narratives, and write a report for each one. The instructor had asked them to write as if they were a reporter of the time period that the book covered. He stated that the instructor wanted to teach them how to express themselves in writing in different ways, but especially in the "historical way."

Romulo stated that three of the required books were historical novels, while the fourth was a slave narrative. He felt that the novels were difficult for him to follow, preferring the narrative, since "it is more straightforward." He felt that it "involves you more, can picture the story better." He generally liked non-fiction over fiction, he reported.

This course also had two graduate assistants who conducted study sessions. He found them very knowledgeable. In addition, he described the teacher as "easy to talk to." He also reported that his wife had taken many history classes in the past and thus had a solid background in it. Therefore, he tried to discuss the material with his wife whenever he could.

Romulo stated that in spite of the fact that it was his major, he actually found his Introduction to Public Relations class boring, because he had taken the class before, "more than once," back in his home country. He felt that he "already understand[s] this stuff." He felt that he "just want[s] to go out and do it." He stated that much of the vocabulary for public relations was the same as in his first language, only with a different pronunciation, but that some of the terms were used differently.

For this course, Romulo reported being required to do a great deal of research and group projects, which he felt would be difficult, given the large number of students in the course. He stated that they had already practiced for the group work by answering questions as a group. The teacher had expressed that she wanted them to form natural groups on their own. He stated that the people in this course seemed to be more open to other cultures than in his other courses.

For this course, Romulo had to read only one book, which he described as having "a different style." He stated that it was filled more with concepts and information about the public relations career than other textbooks, almost as if it were "trying to sell me on the career." Therefore, with only one textbook and with just a few extra handouts, the reading had been "not too bad." He found his teacher to be friendly, stating that she "tries to look tough, but is not really." He claimed that he could tell this about her because of his past experiences on the job. He also stated that he could tell that "she wants to do her job well."

This course required Romulo to write a five page paper, with a due date that was coming up soon. Romulo stated that he planned to talk to the instructor about the grammar of his paper before he turned it in. He wanted the instructor to know that the problems that the paper might contain grammatically came from the fact that he was a non-native speaker of English, not because "I don't know or am stupid." He also planned to ask the instructor to tell him if he had any mistakes, so that he could learn from them. He stated that he felt that it would take years to get good at public relations writing, but felt it was necessary since it was important in his field to have good writing skills.

He reported that there was a great deal of research required for this class. He stated that he would have to do much reading on his own and that the instructor required a wide variety of sources. He stated that the instructor encouraged a "professional approach," which included a portfolio. He believed that he would like this style, based on his past experiences.

Romulo claimed that he liked his Communication Graphics course the best, since he enjoyed using computers. He reported that he had also taken this class in his home country, but that the students there did all of their work by hand, "the old-fashioned way." In spite of his previous experience, therefore, he was unfamiliar with the software required. He wanted to take this course because he believed that it was extremely important to have computer knowledge in his field. Public relations, he said, "means working with technology." He found that his background experiences helped him a great deal to understand the processes that the instructor was teaching them, which allowed him to be able to concentrate on learning how to use the computer software, rather than the concepts that the software was supposed to develop. This made him feel that he could go faster than the others in the class, all of whom lacked any previous background in graphics or public relations.

As mentioned above, Romulo reported finding that the vocabulary used in this class was used differently than he had used it in the past. He stated that he knew the terms, but that they are used differently both in the specialized area of computer graphics and from the way that he was taught to use them in his native language. He reported, however, that the teacher had given handouts with definitions, because others in the class were also having difficulties. He felt that he had to relearn how the terms were used in this special field and how they were used differently from the way that he had used them in the past. He felt that he needed to write down the vocabulary first before he could remember it. He stated that he needed to see it and have the sense of feeling it while it was being written if he wanted to remember it.

As mentioned earlier, Romulo thought of himself as a visual learner. Since this course was done at a computer and "is very hands-on and learn as you do," he felt very comfortable. He reported that the instructor would first model a process to the class, then each student would perform the task independently. He felt that this was the best way for him to learn, since he could see directly how the task was performed and could experience it immediately.

Romulo reported that he would have a final project that would require group work. As a group, the members had to design and produce a magazine. Since this class only had twelve members, he expected the group work to go much more smoothly. He found his classmates to be "open-minded and more professional" and claimed that he learned better in such a situation. He stated that he was now beginning to change his mind about people at The University. He initially felt that people were closed-minded, but that he had now found the people in Introduction to Public Relations and Communication Graphics to be very friendly. People had been inviting him and his wife to dinner and parties, he reported. He found that people in the same major are "much more friendly to you."

Romulo reported that he was surprised at how few people asked questions in the History of Western Civilization and Astronomy classes, but attributed this to the large and intimidating class sizes. He claimed that he was not afraid to ask questions himself, however, even in the larger classes.

The Third Interview

Romulo was interviewed for a third time just prior to spring break. He stated that at this point, "classes are pretty tough." He felt that there was a large amount of material to read and remember. He had three upcoming midterms. He reported that he had begun to use a highlighter and tried to find time to review the highlighted parts whenever he could.

Romulo continued to describe the Astronomy class as "pretty good." His strategy in this course was to take notes, all of which he claimed to remember easily, so he didn't have to read the textbook. He felt that since it was a basic course, the vocabulary was easy and even felt that the course was designed to be easy. He found keeping up with the quizzes to be easy as well, although there were many quizzes and tests, which came basically every week. The instructor had fallen into a set routine, Romulo reported. Class was held twice a week. On the first class period of the week the instructor discussed the subject. Then, on the second meeting of the week, he finished the subject and then gave a quiz over the subject just covered. Romulo liked this because he felt that the information was easier to remember because it was "still fresh." Tests were also easy, he claimed; since they covered the same material as the quizzes, he stated that he had "already had a chance to practice" by the time of the test.

The History of Western Civilization course, Romulo reported, had "too many books to read." He termed the books "tough," with "too many dates to remember." He found the subject matter interesting, but at the same time confusing. The instructor, attempting to interpret history, tried to compare different ages, which made him confuse the different dates even further. This forced him to go back to the book again and see which century she was talking about, which took a great deal of time.

As mentioned previously, however, the instructor did make an outline which Romulo felt helped him greatly when he studied, since he could follow her ideas. He felt that because of the outlines, he did not have to read all of his notes, but could just go over the outline instead.

Romulo reported that he had begun to read the required novels and after spring break he had to hand in a four page essay. His assignment was to write as a journalist of that time period. He stated that "doing the reading in the first place is hard. Doing the assignment is even harder." The first book that he read was a narrative, which was easier to read and managed to keep his interest. He felt that it was "straightforward," since "it goes from past to present." The other books, however, were not so linear, so they were much harder for him to understand. Part of the problem, he reported, was that they used "very old language," which he had never studied before. In addition, the books also assumed knowledge of history that he felt he did not possess. He felt that the textbooks were easier, since they didn't assume this previous knowledge. Also, the teacher told them what specific pages to read, which lowered his reading burden.

Overall, Romulo stated, History of Western Civilization was taking the most time because of the large amount of reading that he had to do. During each class, he reported, he was taking "at least ten pages of notes," which created a great burden. In addition, while he stated that he found the subject interesting and informative, he felt that he wouldn't be using any of the knowledge gained from this class in the future. While it was interesting, he felt that it was a burden, especially when considering the large amount of time and effort he had to put into the class.

Romulo also described his Public Relations class as "tough." He found that a great contradiction existed in this class. He found the material easy to read and understand, having taken similar courses in the past, but found it "hard to understand the way she asks questions." He reported that it had been hard for him to adapt to the teacher's method of questioning and answering questions. He had also found it hard to understand the subtle differences in the way that she used the vocabulary in this course. On quizzes, this gave him problems. In his home country, he stated, the instructor would only be interested in finding out if the students understood the main concepts that had been covered in class, not the smaller details. He claimed that in this class he found it hard to understand which answer to give on a quiz, since the terms "are so similar in meaning." He reported that on these quizzes, the students "must know the exact answer." By asking the students to make fine distinctions between answers, he believed, the instructor was asking him to prove that "he really understands." He stated, however, that while he could easily remember the larger concepts, he had a hard time remembering the exact differences between similar words. Despite the fact that the style of the teacher didn't work well for him, he was doing "O.K." in the class.

Romulo stated that this class required much reading and research as well. He had to write four papers for this course, as well as complete a group project. There were four people in his group, all of whom were international students. The instructor assigned them to the same group. Romulo reported that he liked this situation. Since he had never worked with Americans in a group before, but had had much experience with other international students through the IEP and the language academy that he attended before coming to The University, he felt that this group would be more productive than if he were grouped with American students. He felt that, as a group, the international students in his group understood each other very well. He stated that in America, he found that everyone was assigned individual parts and each did the work on their own. In his country, however, all members would do the work together. They got involved in every part of the project, so "they know everything." If someone got sick, he claimed, the others could fill in and the group would not be hurt. In the American way, he felt, you wouldn't know the project in-depth. In his home country, it was hard to see who was in charge, since everyone had to agree on what to do. In America, you had to have a team leader. In this group project, Romulo had been elected the team leader. He stated that he did not want to assume the responsibility, since he was so busy, but that the other group members persuaded him to accept the role. The others in the group were "too shy," he reported. If a person was willing to be the leader, the others would let that person assume the role, which he felt was very different from the way Americans do it. In America, he felt, all of the members wanted to be the leader. He felt that one of the differences in how groups work in his country versus in America was that in his home country decisions came more slowly, with much more debate. Here, group members were forced to make decisions much more quickly, even if someone in the group did not agree with the decision. However, in America, the group was allowed to revise their project, while in his home country, group members were never allowed to revise. Rather, they "must have it perfect the first time."

For each of the four research papers that he had to write, the instructor generally asked for five sources. Students were instructed to cite two books, a newspaper or magazine, and the internet. They could then choose one more source on their own to supplement the research. He stated that, therefore, he "needs to look everywhere for information." This had forced him to learn where the good sources were for public relations. Research had been difficult, however, because the subjects that the instructor assigned were broad, which forced him to look at "too much stuff." He reported that he had to first take a look at a source, read it, then decide if it was what he wanted or not. This process, he felt, was time-consuming. As a process of adaptation, Romulo reported picking three books that "seem the most interesting" and adapting what he would write about to fit that topic.

Romulo also reported that he had been going to The University's Learning Center, a tutoring center, to get help with writing. The instructor for the class asked them not to work with classmates, since the information contained in the papers was "private," and so recommended the Learning Center as an alternative. He felt that he was learning more about how to write than he had in the past because the feedback was immediate.

In the IEP, he stated, he would hand in a paper, then not get the paper back for several days. Therefore, the feedback was quite delayed. By the time he would consult with the instructor about the paper, he would have forgotten what he had written. He reported that he reviewed his first paper for this class by himself four separate times and received only a grade of "C."

On the second paper, he reviewed the paper only once, this time with the help of the Learning Center tutor, however, and got a grade of "A" on it. Rather than take the paper away to read, the tutor responded immediately to Romulo's paper, explaining to Romulo what his reactions were to his paper and how he was interpreting Romulo's words. Through this exercise, Romulo reported that he could explain to the tutor what he was trying to say and the tutor would then help him find the right words to express those thoughts. Romulo found that he had far fewer mistakes on the second paper than the first, with much less time and energy spent. He also felt that the next paper would be easier because he felt that he remembered the mistakes he had made more easily when feedback was immediate, and could thus avoid them better in the future. This had led him to feel much more confident about his writing.

Romulo reported that he had asked the Learning Center tutor who helped him with his second paper to be his writing tutor for the remainder of the semester and through the summer. He felt that he wanted to continue with the same person because "it is embarrassing to have someone see your mistakes." In addition, this person had experience with public relations and was more of a "specialist" than the others in the Learning Center.

Romulo described his Communication Graphics class as his "favorite class" and was the class where he was "doing the best." He felt that this was mainly due to the fact that he had a good background in this subject, except for the terminology. He stated that he tried to "just forget about the terms" and instead "to use different ways to explain things," which the instructor did not seem to mind. He reported that he could usually understand when the others in the class said something, but he himself couldn't always use the vocabulary actively. He stated that he always understood when the instructor was explaining something. He felt that in this case, vocabulary from his first language was sometimes getting in the way. He felt that if he were to use the vocabulary they use in the class on an everyday basis, for example if he used it for his job every day, it would be easier to remember. Fortunately, he claimed, he was able to recognize the terms when they were used on quizzes. He couldn't say the terms off the top of his head, but stated that he could generally recognize them. He also reported getting help from his wife when he didn't understand a term.

Romulo stated that he liked this class, primarily because he had much more experience than the other members of the class, except in the area of software. Because of his past experience, he was able to concentrate on the class projects, rather than having to focus so much on language as he did in his other courses. He stated that he had a much better understanding of how to create graphics than the others in the class. While his classmates took up to a week on a project and usually had a hard time making the deadline, he was able to give the project to his instructor ahead of time, so that she could "look for mistakes," then he could "fix it up." He reported that the instructor was more than willing to give the extra help needed. She had made it clear to him that she liked this because he was showing that he was working hard and taking the class seriously.

Romulo stated that he needed "to do better on tests after spring break." He felt that he needed a break; after taking a rest, he felt that he would be able to work harder. He felt that he needed to focus on the problems that he had, especially his writing skills, "how to remember things from history," and "how to be efficient."

In retrospect, Romulo stated that if he could change anything, he would have made himself more efficient. He felt that he should have spent more time analyzing what his teachers wanted and how to adapt himself to particular teachers. He felt that he needed to be more efficient about note taking, which he explained as meaning to "not take notes over everything" as he had been doing, but rather to take notes over what the instructor highlighted. He felt that he couldn't focus so much on the words, but rather should focus on the concepts that the teacher was talking about. He had recently been experimenting with making an outline, immediately after history class, over what the instructor covered that day, rather than trying to write down the specific words that she used. He stated that he wanted "to concentrate on ideas, not words."

Romulo felt that an IEP writing class would be better if the instructor and student worked together to go over anything that the student wrote as soon as possible, rather than wait so long. He felt that when the tutor at the Learning Center explained his mistakes to him right away, while they were fresh in his mind, it was the best way for him to learn. In this way, he claimed, he would "never forget the mistake again." He felt that in this way, the tutor was not just helping him create a better individual paper, but helping him learn real language as well. He stated that after the tutor explained something to him, he used the writing as a model for the next time, which he stated "helps get it into my brain easier."

Romulo also stated that when taking his IEP grammar class, his speaking skills were higher than the others, so that he felt that he was sometimes "going backwards." He stated that he felt IEP students needed to learn to express themselves first in speaking before moving on to writing or grammar, and that the IEP needed to put students in groups that were more equal in speaking ability.

He also stated that "tapes don't work for a listening class." He felt that it would be much better to "have a different teacher each week" and that the instructors should "bring in speakers." He felt that his experience had shown him that "everyone has a different accent." The more different people you hear the better, he felt, since you would hear so many different accents in mainstream classes.

The Classroom Observation

The classroom observation for Romulo was conducted in his History of Western Civilization class. This class was a very large class, taking place in a large auditorium style classroom. Every seat in the room was filled, with people sitting in extra chairs against the back wall of the classroom. When I entered the room, an outline of the topics to be discussed that day was on an overhead projector at the front of the class. The instructor and two assistants were standing at the front of the class discussing something as the class settled down. When Romulo entered the auditorium, he went directly to the front left of the classroom, sat down, and began to write down the outline on the overhead in a notebook.

During the course of the class, only about six or seven students out of the one hundred and twenty or more present asked questions or contributed to the discussion. However, these six or seven people, all of whom sat in the general area of the middle-front of the classroom, were referred to by name by the instructor. When asking these people questions, the instructor spoke in a very conversational tone. However, when lecturing, the instructor seemed to be performing as if she were reading a speech. She was very clear and concise in speaking. In spite of the large crowd, because she spoke so clearly, she was easy to understand. The instructor followed the overhead outline point by point, with more specific information given on PowerPoint. She would stop occasionally to allow time for people to catch up writing their notes.

During the course of the class, Romulo did not write down much of what the instructor said, beyond the outline and a few of the notes from the PowerPoint presentation. At the end of the session, the instructor handed out a quiz. This took a great deal of time because of the large amount of people in the room. During this time, the noise level grew appreciably in the classroom. As the session began to near its end, noise from banging doors and people chatting increased greatly.

The Fourth Interview

The fourth interview with Romulo took place two days after the classroom observation. Romulo described the classroom observation day as "a typical day," although he felt that people usually asked more questions than they did on that day and were more involved generally than on that day. He stated that the instructor knew the names of a small number of people and could call on them by name because they were the ones who came to visit her during her office hours and were the ones who were always asking questions during class. All of these people, he claimed, sat up in the front of the class, near the middle, where they would be closest to the instructor.

Romulo stated that he felt that the instructor wanted students to talk back and ask questions. He stated that there was more discussion when they had something extra to read and the students could bring questions from those readings into the discussion. He stated that when they had extra readings, the instructor would usually conduct a class discussion over the readings at the beginning of the class. This had the effect, claimed Romulo, of making the rest of the session more relaxed and loose, leading to better discussion later.

Romulo stated that the instructor, as she usually did, put an outline on the overhead of the issues to be covered in the class that day. He stated that the instructor did this for every class period. He felt that this outline was very helpful in that it told him what terminology would be on the next test, which parts to study, and what was important or not important to remember. He also claimed that it helped him remember the issues better.

Romulo stated that the instructor put the outline up "twenty minutes before the class, so that the students can go there early and copy it down." He stated that he usually didn't come there too early, but since he didn't take too many other notes, he had time to write down the outline. He didn't take many notes, Romulo stated, because "I think if I take notes while she is talking or something like that, I lost the connection with what she is saying." Instead, he preferred "to hear what she is saying. If I know she is talking something I'm not going to remember, I write it down." He preferred to listen to her, he stated, which he believed would help him remember the material better.

Romulo stated that the quiz they took on the observed day covered what they had already read. He stated that the instructor would generally take a week to cover a section. After she was done with that section, she would give a quiz to see that the students had been keeping up with the readings. Usually, Romulo stated, there were three quizzes before a test. Each quiz covered the most important parts of the lectures. He stated, "If you know that and you do well on the quizzes, you're gonna answer all the questions on the test." In this way, Romulo considered the quizzes as a guideline for a test. The first quiz, he explained, would be over the meanings of terms; the second quiz would cover the readings that they had been assigned; and the third quiz would cover the important issues they had been discussing in class. These three quizzes then matched the three parts of the test, which made taking the test easier.

The instructor had informed Romulo that this class was much larger than it would normally be. She had also told Romulo, however, that he was one of only twelve people in the class who asked questions, so she sometimes felt that it was really only a twelve person class. The rest of his classmates' names, she had told him, she didn't even know.

Romulo felt that by asking the instructor questions, he had helped himself because it had helped him to get to know the instructor and "know what she wanted." He felt that by asking her questions, he had let her know that he was not a native speaker and that the way that he expressed himself would naturally be different from the others in the class. In this way, he felt, the instructor could better understand his background, "which is so different." This, in turn, would help him be able to stay level with the others in the class.

Romulo felt that developing this relationship would help him in the end and make his final grade better, since she gave twenty extra points for asking questions. For this reason, he always made a point of sitting in the first row, where the instructor could see him better. He stated that if he sat in the back, he would get distracted. With such a large class, there were many noises and distractions. Therefore, he preferred to sit in the front and to tune out the people behind him, thus hearing more easily and clearly. He stated that he felt the instructor was good at handling such a large number of people and did well in "dealing with all the stuff."

The Final Interview

The final interview with Romulo took place while he was preparing to take his final exams. Romulo stated that the instructor for his History of Western Civilization class had been very helpful before the final test. He reported that she and her assistants had been giving review sessions, which he had gone to. He reported that they "go over all the stuff again," which he found very helpful. He stated that the students "have to ask questions over their notes." If you miss class, he stated, you need to get notes from someone else "so that you know what to ask." He found such study sessions helpful because they told him what was going to be on the test and how the instructor would construct her test. He stated that while they didn't tell him this directly, he felt that he could tell by "what they have to tell you."

Romulo stated that he didn't write that many notes himself. He instead preferred to listen to the lecture and try to grab the main points. Then, when he studied for the test, he went through the outline provided by the instructor and tried to "remember the class." If he didn't remember the specific class, then he would go to the textbook.

Romulo stated that he tried to get the relationship between what the instructor had said and what the textbook said. "The book is a history book," he stated, "so it has time by time." On the other hand, the instructor "is more give you pictures and examples, and helps you keep in mind what it is telling about and gives you examples from today and in the past and how they are related." He felt that in this way, the instructor gave him much more than what was in the book.

Romulo stated that to pass the test, students had to read the book carefully, since the test had three parts. The first part covered meanings of words and sentences said by someone in history. The second part came from the textbook. The instructor would give them a paragraph from some part of the book and the students had to know who wrote or said the paragraph and had to know what the meaning of the passage was or what the author/speaker wanted to say in the passage. The third part of the test covered broader issues. Students had to write a short essay answer from a choice of questions. These questions cover a range from "direct from the book, to her lectures, to your own ideas." He stated that "if you don't read the book, you will first fail the quizzes," and then in turn fail the tests.

Romulo stated that he had finished reading the three extra assigned books, two of which were novels, the other a narrative. He stated that he preferred the narrative style, since "it tells you stuff about what you want to know, but does it without being boring." He didn't read the entire textbook, he reported, only reading the assigned parts, because he found it "boring and dull." He found that reading names and dates was "boring and hard to read."

Romulo stated that his Astronomy class was "so easy, maybe that's why I liked it." He stated that he "didn't touch the book, didn't open it." He also stated that he didn't take any notes during this class, that he "didn't have to, to pass this class." Instead, he went to class every time and paid attention to what the instructor was discussing. In addition, he "watched things on astronomy on the Discovery Channel." He stated that he didn't have any trouble passing the tests since they were relatively easy.

Romulo stated that the vocabulary for astronomy matched the vocabulary from his native language. He stated that he already knew the concepts and terms in his first language, so it was easy to "switch to English." In addition, since the course was a low-level course, the way the course was structured made the vocabulary easy. He stated that "they don't expect you to know too much."

Romulo stated that he felt learning the vocabulary of astronomy was easier because he was always reading about it day to day or "seeing something about it on television." In his other classes such as Communication Graphics, he reported, he didn't hear the vocabulary on a daily basis, and didn't see it unless he was in the classroom or was working with it in the field. He stated that he felt that these were two different ways to learn vocabulary.

In the Communication Graphics class, he won a prize for his magazine design. The instructor had encouraged him to take another graphics class, which boosted his confidence. He stated that near the end of the semester, he finally began to "get the vocabulary," although it took him "until the end of the semester." What helped, he stated, was using it over and over again while practicing on the computer. He felt that he needed to first read about it and then use it in real life.

Romulo, like many of the other informants, had problems dealing with presentations. He stated that after finishing individual projects, he had to speak to his classmates about how and why he did his project the way he did. He reported that the first time he presented, he was scared and worried that they would not understand. With more practice, however, he felt he had gotten better. He stated that presentation work in the IEP would have been helpful. However, he cautioned that everyone in IEP classes was an international student, and "they might understand your mistakes too easy." When you go out into mainstream classes, he stated, you had to "speak with people that it is their language. The way you speak it, you are afraid of rejection. These people are very different."

Romulo related that in the past, he had given speeches to elementary school students through The University's International Student Program. In these speeches, he answered questions that the students had about his country. This "helped to break the fear" for him. Therefore, he felt that the IEP could have its students present in other classes such as history classes or human behavior classes, where they could talk about the differences between countries. Students needed to break their fear, he believed. He felt that the other students in the IEP were "just too nice. They know too much stuff. They know why you make the mistakes that you do."

In his Public Relations class, he had the option to take the final test. He took the test and got an "A", which helped to raise his final grade. He stated that, against his expectations, the instructor got tougher about writing skills. At the end, he was being graded down for every mistake, that the writing now "has to be perfect." Therefore, he had to go to the Learning Center for special help. Because of the help that he received there, however, he stated that he only had to go there one time for each paper before handing it in. He stated that now that he had the "structure part" down and could focus on that by himself, he only had to get help with the "grammar part" from the Learning Center. He was also collecting models to follow, especially for his journalism classes. He stated that the research for his papers went very well, now that he had become comfortable with The University's library system.

In addition to papers for the course, Romulo also had to give a final presentation, which was included as part of his group work. After the presentation, he stated, "I didn't remember anything about what I said. I didn't even know if I was speaking well or if I was speaking [his native language] or what." He felt that group work and presentations almost always go together. He stated that the experience was made easier because he got along well with the people in his group. They all shared similar backgrounds and interests. Only one person in the group was not in public relations, but Romulo felt that that was helpful because this person could see the group work and presentation from an outsider's perspective. He wasn't able "to speak the public relations language," so he asked questions that the other members of the group would not have thought of and was able to point out places where things weren't stated clearly. He stated that for this same reason, he would give his papers to his wife, who was in a different major and could point out places where an outsider would have questions that he wouldn't think of.

Romulo planned to follow his strategy of going to talk to the instructor before the class and explaining that he was an international student. He felt strongly that if the instructor knew this from the beginning, things would go more smoothly for him. He felt that this would let the instructor know that his mistakes were not because he wasn't focusing on the class or didn't care about the class, but rather because he was a non-native speaker. He also felt that with this strategy, rather than marking him down a grade, the instructor would more likely give him help on how to change and improve his papers.

Romulo also stated that he felt that the IEP writing classes needed to focus more on the individual students' majors and the styles of writing in the individual majors. In this way, students "will learn how to write for their majors." He stated that by looking at their majors more closely, students would also find out "how the business moves, what are the companies, who are the people involved." In this way, he felt, he would get "two kinds of knowledge." He stated that he felt very strongly about this because he had found that "the English Department writes very different from the Public Relations or Journalism Departments." He felt that for this reason, writing assignments should be geared more toward what students were going to have to do in the future. Everyone, he felt, had to know how to write in different ways. He suggested that IEP writing instructors "maybe change the style every week" and in this way "help others to know the style of different majors."

Fernanda

"I must not be so shy about what I think... More forceful. Plus, not get angry."

The Background Interview

At the time of the study, Fernanda was a twenty-six year old female graduate student from South America whose first language was a Romance language. She reported that this was the only language that she spoke as a child, both at home and in school. She was a graduate student majoring in Communications. She reported that she had two undergraduate degrees in business, both from universities in her home country, the first in accounting and the second in business administration.

Fernanda stated that she started to learn English in junior high school, beginning at about age twelve or thirteen, where she had a one-hour-per-week English course. She stated that they learned "simple stuff," concentrating mostly on vocabulary such as nouns, verbs, and pronouns. She reported that there was virtually no speaking beyond simple words and phrases. This type of learning continued all the way through high school. At the end of high school, she reported, she could still not speak beyond simple words and phrases such as "How are you?" and "Good Morning." She was able, however, to read simple reading extracts or at least to "recognize many of the words."

She stated that there were about fifty students in each English class that she took and that therefore the teacher could really do nothing more than put words on the board, which the students would memorize, then take a test over.

Then, Fernanda explained, they would "forget about them," since they never had the opportunity to practice them again.

In addition to studying at school, during this period Fernanda also went to a private school for a short time to study English. She reported that she didn't like this study, however. She stated that she had interests other than language and thus convinced her mother to let her drop the English course and take a computer class at the school instead.

In college, she reported, she had "zero English courses." In her university at that time, there were no foreign language courses available to take, she claimed, though her university subsequently offered English and one other Romance language, both of which were elective courses. After graduating from her university, Fernanda spent five years working for a multinational company in her home country.

Before coming to the IEP, Fernanda had a fifteen day traveling experience in the United States, when she visited New York City and Miami, as well as visiting her brother who worked in the city where The University was situated. She reported that she had no need to use English on this trip, however, since they were generally among speakers of her first language. She could also rely on her brother to translate for her.

Fernanda was studying in the United States for the second time. The first time she came to the United States to study was in August, 1996, when she stayed for one and a half years, studying English exclusively at the IEP. Her reasoning for coming to study English in America at that time was that she felt she needed to learn English to move to a newer, higher position within the company that she worked for. She stated that in that company she originally only needed a bachelor's degree to get a good job; later, however, to be promoted, she needed to speak English. She stated that she "knows her job," but that she needed English to go higher in her company. English was a "plus"; you either learned it or you would be stuck at the same level. She stated that in a multinational company such as the one she worked at, they wanted their employees to keep improving, whether it be in languages, computers, or "whatever." She stated that she needed to demonstrate that she had the desire to improve herself and the ability to reach her goals.

After returning to her job after her first experience studying in the United States, Fernanda discovered that if she wanted to go higher in the company or get a better job, she needed not only to speak English, but to have both a master's degree and "life experience" in a different country. Therefore, she returned to the United States in the fall of 1998 to get a master's degree in communications, because she felt that there were many job opportunities in the telecommunications field in her home country and that with a master's degree, she would have more opportunities for advancement.

Economically, the first time that she came to America, she supported herself with the money that she had earned while working. This time around, however, her father was supporting her monetarily. In addition, she was able to live with her brother, who worked at a local hospital. Her brother had been in America for a long period of time and was therefore more familiar with American culture and had thus been able to guide her along very well. She stated that her mother and father were very supportive of her studying in America, so much so that they had even pushed her to do so. Her brother was also supportive of her decision.

Fernanda stated that she spoke her native language at home with her brother and to him outside the home, except when English speakers were present. However, she stated that she did do a lot of speaking in English, since her brother, who was "the only one around who speaks my language," was generally very busy and she was only able to see him for about 10 minutes a day.

Fernanda's attitude toward language learning was that it was fun to learn and it was especially fun to learn the target culture. When she was younger, she stated, she had no interest in learning English, but now was very interested in learning and tried to improve every day. She stated that learning English had helped her understand her own language, culture, and history much more, especially through her contacts with other international students.

As a way to improve her English, she did homework and watched "a lot of TV." She stated that she liked news and entertainment shows. She also liked to "brush up" on grammar by looking through her grammar book repeatedly. She felt that there was simply too much information supplied in any given grammar class and that there was no way to put it all into practice during class time. Therefore, she felt that she needed to brush up whenever possible.

Fernanda's perceived use of English in the future was that she wouldn't need to use it on a daily basis, but rather maybe two or three times a week. She felt that she would be required to read a great deal in English, however, since much of the business correspondence that she would receive in her job would be written in English. She also felt that perhaps she would use spoken English for meetings with visitors or talking on the phone with Americans.

To keep up her level of English upon her return home, Fernanda planned to get a job where she needed to use English. She also hoped to be able to put herself into English-speaking environments as much as possible, such as getting a part-time job helping in a language school and attending conversation groups which meet in local pubs. She also wanted to find a job in a company with "a strong connection" to the United States, where English would play a big part.

Fernanda reported that her current short-term goal was to improve her pronunciation. In an effort to improve, she had been going to the Speech Pathology Department's speech lab. She felt that all aspects of language went together and she needed to learn and practice all aspects, but she felt that she had the most trouble with speaking. She stated that she knew that it would be impossible for her to sound like a native speaker; instead, she just wanted to be able to speak "clearly," especially for any future job that she might get. She also stated that she wanted to improve her "job vocabulary" and hoped to learn a more "formal language" in her major.

The Second Interview

The second interview with Fernanda was held approximately three weeks into the semester. Upon entering the room, the first thing that Fernanda said was, "[Communications] is not easy!' Fernanda was taking three graduate classes: Theory, Management, and Public Issues. She stated that the teaching style in these three classes was very different from that of teachers in her home country.

In the Public Issues class, Fernanda reported that the instructor "speaks too much!" She stated that the instructor talked about important issues, issues that would be useful for her in the future, but that the issues that he talked about were simply "not about public issues." For example, she stated, he talked about "how to be a master's student." He had informed them that "the classroom is not a classroom, it is student-centered training." He informed them that he "is not a professor, [he] is a student-centered trainer." Therefore, the students in this class were to be both students and scholars. He had also informed them that they were there to teach each other. Fernanda felt that this instructor "puts too much on the students." She stated that he pointed to individual students and asked them to tell the class something. In her words, he "puts students on the hot seat." This style of teaching made her very uncomfortable, she stated. The culture of her home country, she felt, was very different. "In America," she stated, "students are taught to ask questions." In her home country it was different; "you only ask when needed." She stated that the instructor for this course refused to accept the phrase, "I don't know." That was not a "master's answer," he had told them. Therefore, the students had to instead answer, "I am not able to answer right now, but I will find out the answer and get back to you." That, the instructor had informed them, was a "master's answer." She felt that this put "lots of pressure on the students." She stated that in her home country, teachers didn't put so much pressure on students. She stated that therefore this class was exhausting.

Fernanda also claimed that students were afraid of the instructor's teaching style because they were afraid that they wouldn't know the information that they need to know to pass the tests. This class was only one section of the course and all sections shared the same tests. The students were also afraid that if they didn't get the information they needed, they wouldn't have enough knowledge to do well in the next class in this series of classes.

For this course, Fernanda had to read three books, plus a packet of reading materials. However, the instructor had told them that "master's students don't read everything." He had informed them that they "must look for key words and be selective and that we shouldn't read everything." However, Fernanda was reading everything anyway. She felt that she had to do this, since she didn't know much about the field and didn't have any background in the subject. Unlike the others in her class, who had been in the program since the beginning of the school year, she began the program at mid-year. This, she felt, put her at a distinct disadvantage in comparison to the other students in her program of study.

She reported that she felt extremely overwhelmed by the first class, so much so that she felt she "should just go back" to her home country. Her classmates told her not to worry, however, and that it would just take a little time. "You will be lost at the beginning," they told her, "but by the end of the semester, you will be fine. Then next semester will be better."

Fernanda stated that she would not feel very comfortable going to talk to this instructor. She did report, however, that even if a student made a statement in class that was clearly wrong, the instructor would never tell them they are wrong. Instead, "he will find something good in it." No one was ever told that they were wrong, a teaching style that she liked very much.

The Theory class, Fernanda stated, was "another tough class, even for Americans." She stated that there was a great deal of information to process, all dealing with laws and regulations. This class, unlike Public Issues, was new to everyone. This class was a team taught class. The first instructor she described as "tough," but said that he was "nice" to her. She stated that she was having a hard time finding a topic for the major paper that she had to write for this class. The instructor, she stated, helped her tremendously. She reported that the instructor loaned her several books from his office and suggested that she pick a topic that she could turn into a specialty, one that would help her find a job. She felt that this instructor had gone out of his way to be helpful to her. He had even offered to read a draft of her paper beforehand, to make sure that she was on the right track. In spite of the help, however, the paper scared her because she was unsure of her topic, which she felt was much too broad. She had been doing most of her research on the internet because it was the most up-to-date, she reported.

During class, Fernanda sat close to the front of the classroom and tape-recorded the lectures. She stated that the Theory class was "tough to listen to," however, since the tapes contained so much specialized law vocabulary, "hard to spell words," and many acronyms. In addition to the major paper, the second instructor, who was the same instructor as the Public Issues class, had students participating in a "think tank" in which they had to, as a group, come up with a weekly newsletter. At the end of the semester, they had to have produced twenty pages.

Fernanda's Management class was also a team taught class, with the teachers switching each week. For this class, there was only one book, the author of which was one of the instructors. She stated that sometimes this instructor was "a little hard to understand" but "is a guy who knows what he is talking about." She stated that he had a lot of management experience. It made her feel confident to realize that he knew his subject well and was a person who spoke directly to the point. She stated that she felt comfortable asking either instructor a question. Both instructors she considered "kind and helpful." Fernanda reported that she was also tape-recording this class.

For this class, Fernanda had to write only one paper, which had to be only eight pages in length. This paper was due near the beginning of the semester, so she was already hard at work on it. The instructor gave the class three options for the paper. She stated that she was getting help from her friends on how to do this paper, since she once again was not sure where to begin.

In addition to the paper, Fernanda had to give a formal presentation, based on the same topic as the paper, sometime after spring break. She stated that she would "lose a lot of sleep" before the presentation. She stated that any public speaking was hard, but public speaking in English was doubly hard.

Fernanda expressed some surprise at the amount of group work she had to do in her courses. She stated that "students here know how to be a team, are more comfortable" with group work. She stated that during the first meeting of the think tank, she "couldn't say anything" while other people freely gave their ideas. She stated that she felt that she would always "be behind the Americans."

The Third Interview

The third interview with Fernanda was held just prior to midterm examinations. Fernanda stated that she was currently "in a hurry to study and read" and was going to bed each night after two o'clock, while she got ready to take two midterms.

In the Theory class, the midterms were causing her a great deal of stress, Fernanda reported. She stated that she got together with others from the class and they put their notes together to prepare for the test. For this class, there was "a lot of stuff to cover." She reported that she had been tape-recording the class, so she had lots of notes. However, the tapes contained a lot of background noise and the instructor's voice was difficult to understand. She stated that she sat close to the instructor, but it was still hard to understand. Some parts of the tapes were fine, she explained, while some parts were not. She felt that it was not just the taping technique, but also that the instructor had "a hard voice to understand" because of its monotone nature.

Fernanda stated that since she had been reading a lot for this class, the vocabulary was no longer causing her so much difficulty. She now realized how helpful taking the previous course in this series would had been, but since she started in the middle of the school year, this was impossible. She felt that the first class in the series would have especially helped with vocabulary. She felt that the other students in the course, all of whom had taken the previous course, were much better prepared that she. However, she stated that handling the vocabulary had become much easier, since she was now more involved in the class.

Fernanda stated that she had been doing a great deal of reading before the test to get ready. This had been difficult, however, since she had many meetings to go to for her group projects. She stated that she had not had enough time to read all of the things that she should have been reading, so she "would have to make it up later." She felt that "they do this on purpose, to put pressure on the students," so that the students could see "what real life was like." The instructor had asked her to read "five or six sections at a time," which she felt was simply too much, so she had become "a smart reader" and had been selective in what she read.

Fernanda reported that her strategy for now was to take notes during class, then fill in the notes with the tapes when she had time. She stated that right now, however, she was only able to keep the tapes, hoping to be able to listen to them later when she finally had time.

Fernanda had a paper due after spring break, so she was planning to spend her break working on that paper. For this paper, she had decided to change topics, since the first one hadn't seemed to work out. She had found the research for this paper to be very difficult. At first, she didn't understand what the instructor wanted her to do. Now, however, because she had had more time and she was more involved in the class and had had more time to think about the issues that the class covered, the assignment was becoming more clear. From being more involved in the class and from doing more reading, things were starting to make much more sense in her mind, she claimed. She reported that the other students in the class had said the same thing to her, that they didn't know where to start either. She felt that she was "now at the place of understanding the class." She stated that during the first stage of the class she was scared, "not because of the English," but because she was so unfamiliar with the context.

In her Management class, Fernanda wrote a paper about gigabits, for which she received a 95 percent. This made her very happy. The instructor gave guidelines that specified six to eight pages, but she wrote twelve pages. She stated that she got some help from a friend on this paper, mainly about ideas of how to structure the paper and how to put the whole thing together. She did all of the research on her own, however, which she found very worthwhile.

In regards to the presentation, Fernanda simply stated, "Oh my God!" At this point, because she had become fairly familiar with the people in the class, she was not too worried about standing up in front of people; however, she was worried about her topic. She was especially worried about the questions that her classmates might ask. She was afraid that most of her classmates, who had been in the program for a longer period than she, would know more about her topic than she did.

In the Public Issues class, Fernanda recently had her first taste of what a formal presentation would be like. Although they had just learned who their "clients" would be the week before, they had to give a presentation the night before the interview. She stated that there simply wasn't enough time to meet with the clients. In the other sections of the class they had more time, and had met with their clients several times, so her section was behind the other sections.

This presentation, which was just one step of many required for the project, was designed to tell the instructor and the clients where the group stood in their project and what they had done. For Fernanda, this was the first opportunity to see what a presentation should be like. Their group had divided themselves into separate subgroups, with each subgroup being responsible for designing one part of the presentation. Then, as a group, they put the presentation together, with the team leader serving as the team spokesman. Fernanda stated that this was a good chance to see how presentations should be structured. Some of the groups read their presentations from PowerPoint, some on overheads, some from notes, some off the tops their heads; therefore, she could see different styles. She felt that she would be able to use this new knowledge to transfer to other classes. For her group's presentation, they only had overheads. The technology part didn't concern her, however; she felt that she had that part down pat. What concerned her were the questions that were asked afterwards.

Fernanda felt that she didn't have much confidence in her team leader. To decide the team leader, students volunteered and then the instructor decided. While she was happy to have him stand up in front, she felt that the instructor made a mistake. In her group, everyone was new to the program except for the person who had become the team leader, while the other groups all had members who were experienced in the program. Therefore, the other groups had an advantage over her group.

Fernanda reiterated that in her home country, there was some group work required, but that it was a different experience from what she had encountered in America. In her time at her university in her home country, she did do a little group work, but not much. As a student in Communications, however, Fernanda felt that she had to adapt to the American style. In Communications, every group had to "act like a company" and "act professionally," she claimed. She stated that she had ideas for the group, but that she didn't state them. She stated that the process had made her feel bad; she had sometimes tried to put her ideas forward, but the others in the group didn't try to understand her, and "basically ignore[d]" her. She put part of the blame on herself, however, since she didn't "push my ideas very hard."

In addition to the presentation, her group had to also do interviews with people who work at their "client's" establishment. She made the suggestion to create the position of "project manager," who would be responsible for parceling out the work and exercising control over what the others had to do. She had noted that other groups had such a project manager. However, once again, her suggestion was ignored. She stated that the group was busy with midterms, though, so she planned to try again later.

Fernanda stated that she was getting some help from other students in the program, most of whom were other international students. She stated that she felt more comfortable getting help from other international students, that she didn't have to ask them for help, since "it just happens." She stated that in her home culture, people were "always helping each other out." She claimed that even if a person didn't know you, they would still offer to help you. Fernanda expressed surprise that people in her program didn't help each other out. She stated that someone could get help here, but only if they asked. This had been a problem for her, because the others in her classes started their program together, so they had already established their relationships with each other before she entered the program. Therefore, she felt like a outsider.

Because of this, Fernanda felt that her department should improve the support structure for international students. She felt that they needed to do more to understand other cultures, but especially needed to do more to help students who were new to the program, since most of them didn't have the technological background they needed to complete the courses. She stated that new students needed more guidance and orientation to the program. She reported that at the beginning, she felt lost, like "a small boat, far, far, far from land." She was quick to add, however, that she didn't want special help; she just wanted to be put on the same level as the students who began the program earlier.

Fernanda stated that her goal right now was to make herself become "more involved" in the project and her classes. At the beginning, she stated, she "didn't know the style it should take, didn't know if I was able. What was the project? I didn't know." She felt that since she hadn't taken the technology classes yet, that she couldn't help much with the project. But now that she was a little more comfortable, she wanted to become more involved. In an effort to do this, she planned to volunteer to be the project manager.

Fernanda stated that she felt that there was a difference in the relationships between teachers and students in America, that they were "at different levels here," while in her home country, teachers and students were at the same level. She felt, therefore, that she had to learn to adapt herself to the way students addressed teachers here, how she should deal with an issue in class, such as a wrong grade on a quiz, and how to treat a teacher professionally.

In retrospect, Fernanda wished that she had taken the International Teaching Assistant course before taking mainstream courses, not while taking them. She believed that this course should be stressed more. As an IEP student, she didn't know about this class, so she felt that it should be advertised to IEP students more, especially to higher level students. She felt that this would help not just for teaching techniques, but for such things as presentations as well. "Even if you are not going to teach," she stated, "it will be good for you."

The Classroom Observation

The classroom observation for Fernanda was conducted during a Public Issues class. When I first entered the classroom, many students were sitting in groups, obviously discussing and planning something. I eventually discovered that all students were members of groups and that these groups were to give status reports on their group projects during the last part of the class. Some groups seemed to be working quite hard at preparing for this. Fernanda introduced me to the members of her group, all of whom were sitting in a row together.

When the class started, the instructor first asked Fernanda to introduce me to the class, which she did by standing up and very formally telling them my name, where I was from, and how she knew me. He also had Fernanda place a name card in front of me. During the course of the class, he addressed them all as "Mr." or "Ms." It was obvious that he wanted to create a very professional atmosphere in the class and that he was modeling for them how to act professionally.

At the beginning of the class, the instructor began by reviewing from previous class sessions, and even got a little information in from previous courses that some of the students had taken. He would say to certain students, "Remember what I said in 601?" The student would then supply the wanted information. Several phrases also kept recurring during the course of the class. One was "value added"; another was "thinking outside the box." The use of these phrases seemed to please the instructor.

During the course of the lecture, the instructor explicitly pointed at people and asked them questions. The members of the class seemed comfortable with this. If someone didn't know the answer, he was not belittling. He would simply ask someone else to jump in and answer the question. It was obvious that he expected others to help that person when they didn't know the answer. He talked a lot about team work during the course of the class. During the class, several students could be seen discussing things with other members of their groups, including Fernanda, who was asking clarifying questions from one of her fellow group members.

During the course of the class, the instructor was very directive about certain things. He would tell the students, for instance, when to write down certain things in their note books that he had said or where to go in the textbook to look for information or passages that he wanted to talk about. His lecture, however, was somewhat difficult to follow, seemingly going off on tangents quite easily. The lecture was easier to follow when he used visual aids, however, and when he was discussing topics from the book. With the visual aids, he followed along with each slide. With the book, he progressed through the chapter, telling students which page to turn to and when to write things down. He also had written a sequence of information on the blackboard and his lecture was easy to follow when he referred to this.

As the class drew to an end, it was apparent that each group was apprehensive about presenting their status reports. However, as the class progressed, there was less and less time left for presentations. Finally, the instructor stated that there wasn't enough time for every group to give their presentations. Therefore, he asked for one group to volunteer. This group went to the front of the class and gave a rather hurried report.

The Fourth Interview

Fernanda stated that in the Public Issues class, the instructor treated the students like professionals, rather than students. He did many things in the class, she stated, that supported that idea. Everyone had to have name plates, which was why he had Fernanda make one for me. She stated that the teacher claimed to be a visual learner, so the name plates helped him learn the individual student's names.

Fernanda stated that students were put into "teams" which remained constant for the length of the semester. Group members were to sit together in class and to study together outside of class. If one of the members of the group had a question, they should not interrupt the instructor; rather they were to ask a member of their team for help. Also, if one member of the team came in late, other team members were supposed to fill that student in on what had been discussed in the class to that point. Therefore, whispering between team members in class was acceptable. The person who was late was also expected to apologize to the other team members for being late. Even if the team carried on work during lectures, she claimed, the instructor would not interrupt them, because they were working as a team. Also, if he asked a student a question and that student didn't know the answer, the instructor would expect another member of the team to jump in and answer for their team member. He had told the class on many occasions, Fernanda stated, that he was modeling "for the real work world."

Fernanda stated that there was a problem for her in her team. She reported that all the members of her group, except for the team leader, were new to the program. She felt that the teacher did not do this intentionally, but rather by accident. He simply had students count off, then put the same numbered students into groups. By coincidence, they were almost all new to the program. Because of this, the other teams had much more experience. She stated that at that point, everyone was doing their share. She felt that the other members of the group, all of whom were Americans, were comfortable working in a team, while she herself was just now getting used to working this way. She stated that she had never had this experience before. She felt that students who came into the program in the middle of the school year were "lost." At the beginning of the school year, she reported, there was an orientation for all new students. At the beginning of the second semester, however, there was no such orientation, so there were many things that students new to the program didn't learn about. The people who had gone through orientation at the beginning of the school year, she felt, were more prepared for the professional atmosphere and team work than those who entered at mid-year.

In addition, Fernanda was involved in a voluntary project outside of her classes. This project was more like real life, she stated, where actual companies came and the groups presented a proposal to them. She stated that she expected group work to get easier in the future as she gained more experience and practice. She hoped that this would be the case, since she knew there would be many group projects in her future. She stated that the instructors in her major encouraged students to act like professionals. They provided students with many opportunities for doing presentations and group work and supported the students in these endeavors.

Fernanda also stated that during classes, the instructor was modeling how to run a meeting, since he noticed that his students were not familiar with how to act and what to do in such a setting. He felt that this was part of professional life, she reported. Therefore, he told them what they had to do and how they should act. He stated that team members should therefore act like they were in a business meeting setting whenever they met. They should have an agenda and plan for what was going to happen next. In this way, the instructor felt that he was not so much treating them like students, but like business people. Fernanda felt that his idea was to teach them how to survive in the business world.

Fernanda reported that the instructor was very happy with the formal introduction that she gave of me at the beginning of class. She stated that the class was usually conducted in such a formal fashion. Students should raise their hands before speaking or when they had "value added" information to give. In this manner, she stated, the instructor was able to "run the meeting and be in control." The instructor had told them previously that if everyone started to speak at the same time, it would be confusing; therefore he asked that students raise their hands and carefully directed who was to go first, second, and so on. All of this was part of the instructor modeling how to run a meeting or seminar. Fernanda stated that the instructor had discussed the difference between a teacher-centered class and a student-centered class on many occasions, and that he wanted students "to teach each other." However, she felt that in spite of his claim that the classroom was "student-centered," the instructor was definitely in control.

Students, Fernanda reported, were not expected to be there just to listen. They were expected to add "something of value" to the discussion. She stated that anything that someone said was looked at by the instructor as a valuable contribution; he never stated that what they had said was irrelevant or wrong. "He tries to find something good in what the person says," she claimed, "to keep something. He tries to find a good thing and add to it." She found this aspect of the class very helpful, since it made the students (herself included) comfortable.

Fernanda reported that at the end of a normal class, the instructor would ask the class how many of them participated in the discussion and asked them to raise their hands. She stated that on most days, most of the people in the class raised their hands, since he did a good job of encouraging participation. She stated that in regards to the ones that didn't raise their hands, he had been doing two things. First, at the beginning of class, as he did in the class that I observed, he asked, "How many people did the assignment?" Those people raised their hands. Then he asked, "How many people did not do the assignment?" Those people then raised their hands. He then told the people who did not do the assignment that they were the ones in charge of the discussion during that class and were responsible for answering questions. Second, at the end of class, he would ask which students participated in that day's class, who "added value" to the class, or said something in class. Fernanda stated that this was done to see the pattern of participation, not to punish those who did not participate. She stated that usually everyone raised their hands.

Fernanda reported that most of the students in the class had had the instructor in a previous course, so they were more familiar and comfortable with him. She felt at a disadvantage this way, since she came into the program in the middle of the year. The others knew his style, she claimed, but she had had to learn this style over the course of the semester. She stated that it had taken her until this point in the semester to get used to his style.

She stated that when he felt an issue was really important, he would say loudly, "I said . . ." and then repeat the information, allowing the students to take notes. In this way, as he did in the class that I observed, he was explicitly telling them when to take notes. She felt that if he emphasized these things, they were important and would therefore be on the test.

Fernanda also reported that for this class, she was to have three different sections of notes. The first section was reserved for any new concepts or words that they studied. The second was for all important citations of materials that he had discussed. The third was for the specific issues that he had discussed in class. She found that the instructor was a very knowledgeable person, but in some ways "knows too much." She found that very often his extra knowledge would overwhelm the discussion, thereby making note taking and following the discussion very difficult.

Fernanda felt, however, that the instructor would be a very good person to work with on a project because she would learn more than just the project; she would also learn how to behave in such groups. Sometimes, she stated, she felt that the material of the course was secondary and that he was teaching more than just the material. He was also teaching a way of behaving.

The instructor could be very organized about the material when he wanted to be, Fernanda stated. When he used the overhead in class, for example, the discussion was very directed, as was the discussion based on the readings from the book. During this period, Fernanda took the most notes and was the most active. She stated that this was because she knew that this was the most important material, not just for the test but for future classes as well.

During the period observed, all groups were supposed to come to the front of the class and give a presentation on the status of their group projects. However, as stated previously, in the end there was only time for one group to present. Fernanda stated that this often happened, that the instructor often didn't leave enough time for planned activities. This bothered her, she stated, since her group had prepared to present that day but was unable to.

A recurring theme in this course, Fernanda reported, was that master's students should be able to find meaning from a book or article without reading the whole book or article. She reported that he often asked, "Do you have to read the whole book?" to which they had to answer "No!!!" He encouraged them to read for key words and phrases. "That," he said, "is the job of a master's student."

One negative aspect of this class, Fernanda found, was that there was a great deal of competition. She felt that through the creation of the professional atmosphere, the department had been creating this competition. She felt that for many international students, this sense of competition would feel "strange." She stated that because of this heightened sense of competition, she felt that she "can't trust anyone." She felt that it appeared to be teamwork on the surface, but was competition underneath, usually competition to get the instructor's attention. She stated that she felt that many of the things that people did were "not real." She stated that the idea of teamwork and group work was a great idea, but that in this atmosphere of competition, "the whole thing is fake." She claimed, "It's not the real me." Because of this atmosphere, she was feeling a great deal of tension as the semester neared its end.

The Final Interview

The final interview with Fernanda took place after she had finished her final examinations for the semester. Fernanda stated that she had recently been told that she would have an assistantship for the next academic year, thereby lessening her economic burden greatly. This had made it easier for her to concentrate on her classes and finals.

She reported that she took her Theory class final exam early. This final "didn't go so good," she stated. Two different sets of tests were given for this exam, she reported, "one white, one pink." She got one of the white ones. She stated that it was "terrible" because she felt that the pink set was easy, while the white set was difficult. Everyone who had a white test complained about the difficulty of the test.

This test, according to Fernanda, was made up of a true/false questions section, a multiple choice questions section, and an essay questions section. She stated that the true/false and multiple choice sections were easy. It was the essay section where she had difficulty. Her response was "ugh!" She stated that she didn't even begin the last question, since she didn't know how to answer it. Many other people in the class, she claimed, left this question blank. When she told her instructor that she had done poorly on the test, however, he told her not to worry.

Fernanda stated that in her Theory class she still had not received her major paper back and didn't expect to, since she believed the instructor kept their papers in a file. She didn't feel confident about the final product, but was "happy to be finished with it." She stated that many people in the course were not sure what the teacher expected of them. She said that "they were kind of lost." They didn't know what kind of notes they should write, for example. She stated that the instructor did give them guidelines, but the guidelines weren't much help.

Fernanda stated that it took her "until spring break to get used to this teacher's voice." It was at this time that they then switched teachers. Fortunately, the new instructor was the same teacher as Public Issues, which made the transition easier.

Fernanda stated that it also took her some time to get used to the use of acronyms in the Theory class, but they became easier as she became more familiar with them. Before she entered the class, she stated, she "didn't have any idea about acronyms." She stated that much of the vocabulary in graduate school took her a long time to get used to, but "sometime after spring break" she began to get comfortable. Now she felt that her vocabulary was "building up quickly."

Fernanda also had some trouble on the final for her Management class. On her final, she reported, there were two questions that she couldn't answer because she had not studied that material at all. She stated that this was her mistake. The two questions were from a chapter of their textbook, a chapter that the instructor for the course had written. "So of course it was on the test," she stated. However, because he hadn't covered the subject in class, she didn't study it. She stated that she had planned to study it later, but didn't have time to cover the extra material. She stated that she was not worried, however, because she had "good grades" going into the final.

The greatest problems that she had experienced, Fernanda reported, were in the Public Issues class. She stated that one of the reasons why she did poorly on her Theory class final was that on the day before the test she had had her final Public Issues group presentation. She stated that the group had "from spring break until the end of the semester" to work on the project. However, when the instructor gave them the project, the other members, Fernanda claimed, said, "It's O.K., don't worry. Everything's gonna be fine. Blah, blah, blah." She stated that she was expecting too much from this project. Since it was her first project, she wanted to see "what they do, how they do."

Fernanda felt from the beginning, however, that the instructor was approaching the groups incorrectly. As mentioned in an earlier interview, the instructor had put students who were all new to the program in her group, with only one experienced member. In her opinion, the experienced and inexperienced members should have been more evenly distributed. In this way, she felt, the experienced members could have "passed on their knowledge to the inexperienced ones."

As the semester progressed, Fernanda reported, the members of her group procrastinated and didn't do any work. They only did "a little bit here, a little bit there." They kept saying, she claimed, "It's gonna be easy." The team leader met the "client" once at the beginning of the project. The group was supposed to give out surveys and to conduct interviews with two employees.

At that point, Fernanda suggested that they approach their client's contact person one more time before giving out the surveys or conducting the interviews. She told him, "We have to tell them that we are going to do the interviews, otherwise the supervisor won't allow it. The employees would be scared to answer questions. Besides, it is not professional to go to do something without authorization." However, the team leader ignored her suggestion, and the other members of the group tried to talk to the employees and to give out surveys.

However, the employees gave the surveys to their supervisor, who wrote on the surveys that "they should contact the public relations department."

Fernanda stated that she "wasn't feeling too good about the group" at that point. The due date for the presentation was on a Thursday, but it wasn't until the Monday immediately before that they finally started to write the final report. The leader told her that she should write the "results" section. Using what she had learned in her IEP advanced writing class, she wrote the part. However, once again, the team leader ignored her contribution. "He didn't even take one sentence from it," she claimed.

Because of the hurried nature in which they conducted the research, Fernanda complained that the final report didn't have enough details, such as how many people were surveyed. She told the group that the readers needed to "have a clue about what percentage you are talking about. 80 percent? 70 percent?" However, one of the other team members said to the team leader, "She is correcting you!" Fernanda stated, "I told him I'm not trying to say that you are wrong. I'm just telling you what I learned in my writing class. Maybe my book was wrong. You don't have to change anything if you don't want to."

Because of their reactions to her suggestions, Fernanda became very angry, and she decided "to take a step back and see what the group would do." After that, she reported, she didn't contribute to the final presentation. She also made up her mind not to go to the final presentation. She decided instead to write a message to the instructor telling him that she was sick and would stay at home studying for the exam the following day.

At noon on the day that they were to present, however, Fernanda received a phone call from the instructor at her home saying that there was a problem with her team. He had gotten a message from their client's contact person saying that she hadn't heard from their team in a long time, that they had met with her only once, and that it wasn't actually the whole team, just the team leader. Therefore, she had assumed that the project wasn't in progress anymore.

Fernanda reported that she then told the instructor that she "didn't know what was going on." She told him that the team leader had met with the group, then given them instructions about what to do. He had divided up the team into two groups which were to do separate parts.

The instructor told her, "This is not correct. This is not what a team should do."

Fernanda responded, "I cannot say anything to you right now. I don't know and I cannot speak about something that I don't know. Maybe you should talk to the team together." She stated that everything that she wanted to tell the instructor would put blame on other people, but that she wanted to be fair and didn't want to talk about people when they were not there to defend themselves.

The client's contact person had informed the instructor that she didn't know that there was a presentation that day, although the team leader had told Fernanda that the contact person knew about it. The contact person informed the instructor that she hadn't known about the presentation until earlier that day and wasn't planning on coming to the presentation, since she had already scheduled a different meeting.

The instructor then told Fernanda, "This is one thing that has to be fixed. You have two and a half hours." Therefore, Fernanda tried to call the other members of her team, but was unsuccessful, so she went to the campus to try to find them. She also had to meet with the contact person and apologize. The actual presentation, according to Fernanda, was "awful." The team, she stated, simply "didn't work the way that it was supposed to." The instructor told her that it was "group work," rather than "team work," and that he didn't want to see "group work" from them ever again.

Ultimately, Fernanda felt, it was not the instructor's fault that the group performed so badly, since he had laid out the guidelines quite clearly. She felt that much of the blame lay with the team leader, who was the only one with experience, and should therefore have directed them in a different way. She also blamed herself, however, since she got so upset with the team members when they were not open or accepting to her ideas.

Fernanda reported that she was well aware that she would have to do group work in the future. She stated that she planned to approach group work differently in the future, however, by trying to work sooner, right from the beginning of the assignment and not put anything off. Even if there wasn't anything specific to do, she believed, they should still get together regularly as a group and do something. If they "don't accept my ideas" or if her ideas "don't get through to them," she felt that she "must find a way that they could understand me." She was afraid, however, that the other members of her group may have rejected her ideas and suggestions because she was an international student or because she was the only female member of the group. She also said that she "didn't demand or force" her ideas. She stated that she was uncomfortable with doing that. Instead, she stepped back and got angry. She felt that in the future, any group that she was a part of needed to be professional, but this group wasn't. The other teams, all of whom had several experienced members, were professional, she felt. She said that she would suggest to the instructor that in the future he divide the experienced and inexperienced members evenly. She stated that this was more like the situation that they would find when they got to their "real jobs."

Fernanda also stated that she felt the IEP should try to simulate teams, "either in writing class or reading class." She stated that students "need to practice getting ideas across." They "need to practice contact between teammates, how to do it right, how to be professional." She also felt that they had to learn to deal with people that they didn't like. She quoted her Public Issues professor, "You aren't going to marry them, you just need to get along."

Fernanda stated that one problem with the IEP was that the other students were also international students. However, she thought that, initially at least, this could be a good thing. She felt that this would be a "good, comfortable chance to practice." Then, as the semester progressed, she suggested, IEP instructors "should bring in more Americans, maybe people from the English Department."

She stated that the longer she was in her graduate program, the better she got to know her instructors and the better she got to know her fellow students. This, in her words, "makes you feel better, makes you feel like someone's there, not just a body."

Fortunately, Fernanda reported that she did have a positive group work experience in her Theory class. In this class, the students were required to produce a weekly newsletter, which went very well. At the end, each group had to summarize how their work on that project went and had a final contest. For the contest, they had to decide on and nominate, as a group, the person who wrote the best article, whose article had the best content, and who had the best style of writing. She stated that she wasn't expecting to be nominated for anything, but ended up being nominated in three categories, in the end placing second for the best content.

Fernanda stated that this was a good group work experience for her. The difference, she felt, was that the group was "more serious and understanding." The other project, she stated, took too long to get started. Any project, she now felt, needed to start right from the beginning. Everyone was responsible in this group, she stated, therefore it was "real team work."

In the future, Fernanda therefore planned to work harder at the beginning of the semester and at the beginning of projects. She stated that she also planned to "not be so shy about what I think. I have to put my ideas for these teams in a better way. Not so shy. More forceful. Plus, not get angry."

During the summer, since she would not be going to school, Fernanda planned to read as much as possible, especially textbooks for future classes. She reported that she needed to read twelve books just for one class that she planned to take during the fall semester. She stated that one thing that would make things easier for her was the fact that two of her teachers would be the same as the current semester, so she would be much more familiar with their styles and voices during the following semester. She stated that she also wanted "to take things in a more professional way" in the future.

Fernanda felt that her IEP writing class "was wonderful" and covered the things that she needed to know. She stated that she felt that IEP reading classes should focus more on reading books from the students' majors to "get familiar with the vocabulary." She used the Theory class as an example. She stated that since she came from a different country, she was not familiar with United States laws and ways of speaking about laws. By reading the text, she felt, she would have been more accustomed to the vocabulary, which would have made the class easier. She also thought that there should be an added "reading with presentation" combination.

Fernanda also stated that she would have liked to have had practice taking notes from lectures as a student in the IEP. However, she cautioned that the lectures should not come from IEP teachers, since "the students are too used to the teacher's voice." Instead they should be "someone different, someone new." She also felt that students should practice giving speeches and presentations to get used to the way of speaking in front of an American audience. She felt that this should include not just the speech itself, but also should cover visual aids and answering questions.

Lyn

"Students had better learn the situation that they will be going into, so they are more prepared."

The Background Interview

At the time of the study, Lyn was a thirty-four year old female graduate student from Asia, majoring in Computer Science. Before coming to the United

States, she earned a bachelor's degree in Public Administration from a university in her home country.

Her first language was an Asian language. Both her mother and father spoke that language, with her mother also speaking another local dialect of that language. She stated that she spoke only her first language at school, though many of her classmates spoke the local dialect. She stated that she did know a little of the dialect, since her maternal grandparents spoke only the dialect and if she wanted to converse with them, she had to learn some of the dialect.

Lyn began studying English in middle school, in "the seventh grade, age twelve or thirteen," where she studied English for four hours a week. She stated that the class consisted of "lots of vocabulary and grammar study." Students were expected to read aloud from a book a great deal and do a great deal of reading on their own. She stated that there was not much speaking involved in the class. The four-hour-a-week class continued through high school with much the same style of teaching throughout. For one semester in high school, however, she also had an American teacher who came to the class and taught them some speaking, as well as American songs. While in high school, she also went to a special school for about three months to learn writing from an American teacher.

Lyn stated that English was one part of the entrance examination that she had to take to be admitted to college in her home country. She also continued to study English for the first year of college. This class was taught in essentially the same style as the high school class, although a listening component was added, since her college had listening equipment, while her high school did not. She stated that in high school, they had listened to tapes "only one or two times."

Lyn stated that her attitude toward English when she first started learning it was positive. She stated that she liked English and liked to read and write in English. She also liked to listen to the American songs that her brother collected. By the time she entered high school, however, she began to dislike studying English because of the large amount of vocabulary which the students had to memorize and produce for the tests. She stated that in college, however, where the pressure was much lighter, she again began to like learning English.

Lyn was different from the other informants in the study in that she had been in the United States for over twelve years, coming originally with her husband who came to attend college in America. During that twelve year period, her husband graduated and got a job at The University. In the meantime, Lyn stayed at home and raised their two children, who were ages seven and five at the time of the study. She stated that since they were old enough at that point to go to school, she had begun to study at The University. She was quite unsure of how her studies would go, since it had been a long time since she had studied formally and because she had almost no background in her major, other than taking "one or two computer classes twelve years ago" in her home country.

Lyn stated that she entered the IEP only because it was required of her before she could begin studying at The University. She reported that her attitude at the beginning was negative, but after taking classes for awhile, she began to realize that it was good for her to take these courses and had begun to develop a positive attitude.

Lyn stated that she was studying English in the short term primarily "to get through school." Her perceived use of English in the short term was primarily for speaking, since she felt that she would have to do group projects in the future. In the long term, she knew that she would have to use English in her future job.

Lyn stated that her husband was very supportive of her decision to study because he wanted her to be able "to find a good job in the future." She reported that her two children "were not too happy for the first few weeks" of the semester that she began at the IEP, but were "now O.K. with it."

Lyn's short-term goals also included working on her listening and writing ability. She felt that she would have to listen to lectures, so listening would be very important. She stated that vocabulary would play a big part in her future. She also felt that "writing homework" would be important.

In the long-term, Lyn hoped to be able to write letters and make phone calls to friends in English more easily and fluently. She stated that she even hoped to use English at home, since her children were quite Americanized. Her current plan was to work on the specialized vocabulary of her major first, then move on to the personal aspects of language learning later.

Lyn's strategy for accomplishing this was to do as much reading as possible. She stated that she liked to read magazines and newspapers, which she found very helpful in learning new vocabulary. She also watched television every day, especially the news programs. She stated that she liked television "for the culture." On the other hand, she stated that she didn't really read English "just for fun," but rather always read for a reason, namely to improve her English.

Lyn stated that her husband had helped her tremendously in the transition to return to school. She felt that she did experience culture shock when she first came to America, but not as much as her husband, who had had to go to school immediately after arriving in the country. She herself had had twelve years to get used to the environment. She also stated that she had American friends living near her in student housing when she first came to the United States, as well as other students from her home country, who helped make the transition more smooth. She felt that her interaction thus far in school with native speakers had been limited, but she stated that she did have extensive contact outside of school, since she had been "running my household here for twelve years."

Lyn claimed that she didn't worry too much about listening or speaking. Her primary concern was with writing. She also didn't feel very confident about reading, feeling that she read slowly and had trouble with vocabulary. She felt comfortable with her speaking and listening abilities, mostly because her major was computer science. She felt that she really needed "to work on my vocabulary," though. She stated that since she was older and had had a great deal of experience living in America, she had developed the ability not to feel embarrassed if she didn't understand something, and just asked for the information to be repeated. When she was younger, however, she got quite embarrassed.

Lyn stated that she felt she didn't have any research skills, but was not worried about this because she was in computer science, where she felt research wouldn't really play much of a role. In addition, she stated that she had her husband to turn to for help, if needed. She felt that she was not good at note taking, but if the teacher wrote on the board, she expected that she would have no problem.

Lyn stated that she felt that her questioning ability was sufficient. She felt that if she could figure out "how" to ask questions, she would not be afraid to ask. Now that she was older, she was not so afraid. Figuring out "how" was a problem, however. She also stated that she was not very organized, which concerned her somewhat.

The Second Interview

The second interview with Lyn took place about four weeks into the semester. Lyn stated that classes were going "O.K..". She was taking three classes at that time. The first was a Computer Science class, while the other two were math classes: Calculus and Linear Algebra.

Lyn stated that her Computer Science class was "not too good" and that there was "not enough time to read. That is the biggest problem." She claimed that she hadn't had enough time to read the parts of the textbook that she had been assigned. In addition to the large amount of reading, she also stated that she "reads pretty slow." Additionally, she reported, the teacher in this class "speaks too fast. Sometimes I just couldn't catch up to what the teacher is talking about." She stated that the reading was not so difficult for her, it was just very time consuming.

This was the first computer programming class that Lyn had taken at The University, although she did take an Introduction to Computers class. At the beginning, the reading was difficult, but after the first few reading assignments she got used to it, so it was not so difficult anymore, she claimed. The problem for her, she felt, was "just time." She had to get used to the style of the textbooks and get into the class for a little while before things started to get better. She found that reading the book "a couple of times" had helped her tremendously.

Lyn stated that in addition to the textbook that they were then covering, she had another book to get through before the end of the semester. Because of the large amount of material to be covered, she reported, the teacher talked very fast. Other international students in the class were also having trouble keeping up with the instructor's speech, especially the ones who "have just come over from other countries." She felt, however, that if she could just read the book and keep up with the readings, everything would work out fine.

Currently, Lyn was taking notes during the class. She stated that she could catch some of what she needed from the notes, and could "figure out the rest from the book." She claimed that the book told her most of what she needed to know to write a program. The instructor's lectures, she believed, added to the book, giving extra examples that helped them to understand the program. When the book didn't explain well, the instructor would add examples. In addition, the instructor was also placing extra materials and examples in the computer labs. These, she felt, would help her greatly, but also take up a great deal of her time.

Time, Lyn reiterated, was by far her biggest problem. She stated that she was not enjoying the class, but felt that if she could catch up, she would enjoy it more. She believed that she "must find the time to read, even if it means less sleep." She stated that she could sometimes do homework during the week, but mostly she did it during the weekends.

Lyn reported that in addition to going to school, she had to take care of her two children. Family life got in the way and it was hard to find the time to do the required reading. Her family was taking much of her time, especially this semester. She was only taking classes in the morning because her children were at home in the afternoons. She stated that it bothered her not to talk to her children when they wanted to talk. This made it difficult for her to concentrate. Computer programming, she stated, "takes time in front of a computer." She had to come to school to do this, however. Therefore, she usually used Sunday afternoons to come to school, the time when her husband could take care of their children.

Lyn noted that she was rather uncomfortable asking the instructor for this class for any extra help, since the instructor was extremely busy and usually had people waiting in line to see her. Additionally, Lyn didn't really have time to wait in line. Instead, she said that she was more comfortable asking her classmates for help. She stated that she usually asked for help from students who knew more about programming than she did, usually people who were from her home country. She also felt more comfortable asking the lab assistants for help, since the interaction was one-to-one and in front of a computer where she could explain her problems more clearly and easily.

Lyn reported that she had a previous class in calculus in high school, but the Calculus class at The University had added more material than she previously covered, especially more formulas. She felt that this high school background had prepared her well, however, and that she liked math, so these two things had made this class the most enjoyable for her.

Lyn stated that almost all of the information that she needed for this class came from the textbook or from what the instructor wrote on the board. If she couldn't get all that she needed from the textbook, she stated that she would go ask a friend, usually another person from her home country who had a background in mathematics. She stated that it was very helpful to go to talk to others from her country, since they were "more easy to understand" and "could explain in more detail." She stated that the instructor for this course was "a nice guy, willing to help" so she also felt comfortable talking to him if she could not understand on her own or if her friends couldn't help her out.

Although it was a math class, in the Linear Algebra course, the greatest problem for Lyn at that point was word definitions. She stated that she had taken "a little bit of algebra in high school," but not enough to help in this class. Therefore, the definitions posed a problem. She stated that there really wasn't that much reading for this course, but the reading that she had to do was filled with definitions. The instructor, she stated, would write a definition on the board, then give an example, and "that's it." If the example was not a good one, she felt lost. She found that the definitions were hard for her to remember and were confusing when there were so many of them at one time. She stated that "if you can't totally understand the book, it is useless." She reported that the other international students in her class felt the same way. She felt that the native English speakers in the class didn't have this problem. She stated that this situation was probably because the teacher was "young and inexperienced." She stated that she would feel comfortable talking with him about this problem, but she couldn't "match his time" to meet with him.

Once again, Lyn stated that time was her biggest problem. The Computer Science class took a large amount of outside-the-class work, especially in the lab. If she couldn't figure out a program, it took "a long, long time," so this was her main problem at that point. She felt that she first had to catch up with the reading, so that she could then complete her computer programs. The math homework, on the other hand, she could do at home, which made life a little easier.

Lyn reported that listening was a problem in two of her classes, Computer Science and Calculus. She stated that there was virtually no writing involved in the classes that she was currently in. She stated that she had to take a great deal of notes in her classes, but this was fine because the instructors in all of her classes wrote so much on the board that notes were no problem. In Calculus, however, she did have some problems reading the instructor's handwriting. She stated that she was not required to do much speaking at all in any of her classes. She did state, however, that she would have liked to ask some questions, but didn't always know "how to ask the question." She stated that she wouldn't be too shy to ask if she knew what she wanted to say.

Lyn expressed surprise at how frustrating the Computer Science class had been. She stated that the introductory computer class was "too easy," so that this class was a big jump. She stated that the instructor expected the students to know a great deal. She felt that she didn't spend enough time at the beginning of the semester studying and reading, which had put her at a disadvantage. The first few classes were frustrating, she explained, and "makes you want to give up." But if she could get over the first hurdle, she believed, everything would be fine. She stated that she just "needs lots of time."

The Third Interview

The third interview with Lyn took place just prior to spring break. It was obvious at this point that Lyn was under a great deal of stress. She reported that her youngest child had been sick. He had been having chest pains and couldn't breathe. This had taken much of her time away from reading and study and caused her great worry. She now had the added stress of waiting for the doctor's results.

The Computer Science class, she stated, was "hard, hard," shaking her head. She asserted that she and the other international students in her class had trouble with the teacher because the teacher spoke "really fast." Partly this was due, Lyn felt, to the large amount of information that had to be covered, part was just the teacher's natural pace. Since the last time we had met, Lyn had caught up on her reading. There was not much reading now, she reported, just a great deal of programming. She reiterated that she wished she had done more reading at the beginning, so that she would have had more time for writing programs.

As in the last interview, Lyn stated that she had to spend much of her time in a computer room, typing and compiling. She was still doing this work primarily on Sundays, when her husband was able to watch their children. Her computer at home was now hooked up to The University's system, but she stated that she still preferred to come to school to do the work because at school she was able to ask for help from others if she had any problems. She continued to ask for help from other people from the same class or from other students from her home country that she knew had already taken the course. In addition, she also went to the Learning Center and found the lab helpful because there was always someone to provide assistance. Therefore, she felt, she was getting a wide variety of help. She stated, however, it usually came down to her spending time in front of the computer by herself, trying to figure the program out. She stated that she was still having trouble connecting with the teacher, since their schedules did not coincide.

Lyn stated that the instructor was now adding much more information to the class than was contained in the books. The instructor put this information on the board, so Lyn had no trouble adding it to her notes. Most of the information was in the form of formulas, so it was easy to follow. Note taking in this class, according to Lyn, was no problem, the teachers notes being easy for her to follow.

Lyn stated that she still had problems with the programming, however, because the teacher did not always explain well how they should write a given program. In addition, the questions were "just too hard to understand." She reported that the other international students in the class felt the same way. Because the questions were so difficult to understand, she didn't "even know where to begin."

The Calculus class, unlike the Computer Science class, had become "quite easy." Lyn stated that the teacher had begun to help the students to a much greater degree, always making sure that everyone in the class knew what he was doing and making sure they all understand what he was talking about before moving on. She reported that he explained step-by-step, stopping frequently to ask the students if everyone was following his explanation. She found that at this point in the semester, she was "understanding [the instructor] much better" and was "getting used to his language and style."

Lyn stated that one or two people in the class raised their hands frequently, which helped the less confident students, such as her. This class also dealt with many formulas, so it was also easy for her to follow, since it was not dependent on English. In this class, like in her other classes, if she had trouble understanding, she generally sought out others from her country to get advice. She stated that because they could explain an answer in her first language, she was able to understand much more deeply. She also felt that the students from her home country had a good background in this area.

Lyn stated that Calculus was easier than Algebra because "you just have to understand what's going on." Algebra, however, required more than just memorization to understand what the instructor was talking about. In Algebra, you couldn't just understand the formulas; you also had to understand the theory behind the formulas, she believed. This was a part of mathematics that she claimed to be unfamiliar with before taking this class.

At the beginning of the Linear Algebra class, she stated, she was not used to this style or used to thinking from a theoretical point of view in a math class. Although she had taken Algebra classes before, studying it in this way was "just not in my background." She stated that she had to memorize what she had learned, then take what she had learned and apply it to what she had learned in the past, then later to what she would learn in the future. It was, in other words, a compilation of all the things that she had learned. The definitions, formulas, and theories, she stated, "all go together."

Therefore, even at this point in the semester, there were still many definitions that she had to learn, she reported. These definitions were getting easier now, however, since they essentially built up off each other. Once again, however, Lyn stressed how important the need was to do well at the beginning of the course, since each definition did build off the previously learned ones. She found that the middle of the semester was much easier, after catching up with all the reading.

The Linear Algebra class, Lyn felt, still posed an "English problem." She often didn't understand what the homework questions were asking. She stated that it was hard to understand "the language of linear algebra." She felt that she still didn't know the specialized language that she needed. This had the effect that "most of the time I don't ask questions, because I am not quite understanding the whole thing that is going on. It is hard to know how to ask." She added, "Many international students don't know how to ask questions, how to interrupt," so they didn't speak much in class. "It is culture," she declared.

Lyn also stated that she felt that the instructors didn't always respect international students, "especially [her home country] students." She stated that when these students went to ask a question, the instructor "doesn't have expression." With American students, she claimed, they "have expression, look happy." She stated that, in spite of this, she wouldn't have any problem asking questions, since she was older and no longer cared what people thought of her. However, she restated, she didn't know how to phrase questions. Students from her home country, she stated, if they are unsure of how to ask a question, would remain silent. "It is," she reiterated, "a cultural thing."

In retrospect, Lyn felt that she should have worked harder at the beginning of the semester and not fallen behind. She stated that if a student worked hard at the beginning, this would help ensure that "the middle and end are O.K." In her case, she had had to spend too much time catching up, which hurt her in the middle. Having "more time in the day" would have been nice, she also stated.

The Classroom Observation

Lyn was observed during her Computer Science class during the week following spring break. During this class, which was held in a small computer lab, all the students sat at computer terminals. Lyn sat near the door of the lab. All the other students around her were also students from her home country.

The instructor began to lecture almost as soon as she entered the room. The instructor spoke rather loudly and rather quickly throughout the entire class, although the classroom environment was small and tight and not particularly noisy otherwise.

During the course of the class, the instructor wrote an amazing amount of what I assume was a computer language on a white board with a highlighter. She did not have the overhead computer screen as I had seen in many other classrooms. She didn't seem to be referring to any notes, but rather spoke off the top of her head. The information that she wrote on the whiteboard came quite rapidly. The information that she wrote took the form of "First do this. Next, you would see this. When this happens, then do this. After, you will see this." This rapid fire flow of information continued throughout the class observed.

In the meantime, as the instructor was writing notes on the whiteboard, students would respond accordingly on their computers when instructed. On three different occasions, Lyn referred to the person next to her, a female from her home country, to find out what she was supposed to do. The other person provided the necessary input. Others around this person also referred to her.

In addition to the instructor, two other assistant were in the class. They would walk around among the students, looking at their computer screens. Occasionally, they would make suggestions to the students, although they only made one suggestion to the group of students from Lyn's home country who sat together. At the end of the class period, most of the students left, but Lyn's group all stayed and worked together.

The Fourth Interview

Lyn stated that her Computer Science course was difficult. She stated that the instructor spoke very fast and very loudly. Lyn no longer believed that this was so that they could cover the amount of material they had to cover during the semester. Rather, she now believed that this was just the natural way for the teacher to speak. She had a hard time keeping up with the pace of the instructor, however, because of the speed and the amount of information that was given out in each class session.

One of the biggest problems, according to Lyn, was that while the instructor did give them examples, these examples "are not enough." She felt that as the class got harder, there was not enough extra information from the class. She compared this class to her Calculus class, where the instructor gave many examples and didn't move on until everyone understood the material. Also, the things that the instructor covered in class did not coincide with the things they had been reading in their textbook, so she felt the students "don't know how to do the real projects."

Lyn stated that there were many projects required for this class. She stated that it was hard to finish all the projects. She stated that it was not just inputting the data, but how to do the programs that was giving her so much difficulty. She felt that most of the people in the class were not very good at computer science, so they had to take a long time to finish the projects, which put them behind in other classes. Just like her, the others in the class had no background in computer science either, so they had similar problems.

For this class Lyn had to spend a great deal of time in front of a computer, "getting a program to run, getting everything to work right, getting the right answer." Then, after all that, she had to study for the test. Some programs were hard, she stated, because "you can't figure out what is wrong," then she had to spend a great deal of time trying to locate the problems. It wasn't like other courses, she felt, where you could just sit down and study.

Lyn was not happy with the way her programs were turning out, so she got help from another student in her class who was from her home country. They worked together on their projects, she reported. This person, she believed, was "much better than the others," so the members of the class asked her for her advice on how to do the programs. This person was very helpful. Lyn stated that this person was "younger, so she understood much better."

Lyn also stated, however, that she had spent too much time getting help, and not enough time thinking for herself. She felt that she needed to learn how to do these projects on her own and to think through projects by herself. She stated that she needed to do things by herself and figure out problems, so that she "can get used to the idea."

The Final Interview

Lyn was interviewed for the final time just after finishing her final examinations. Lyn stated that all of her finals went fairly well. She stated that she still didn't know what grade she received for her Computer Science class, but felt "the test went O.K." She felt that it went fine because it "was not very hard." Most of the material, she stated, had already been covered in previous exams. She felt that the teacher was being "nice" at the end of the semester.

Once again, Lyn stated, she didn't have enough time to do all the reading she felt was necessary to fully prepare for the exam. Mostly, she stated, she followed the notes she had made in class and tried to practice the programs, although she found this very time consuming. She reiterated that the examples the teacher gave were not sufficient.

Lyn stated that she was planning to take more computer language classes in the fall, so she felt that she really needed to try things on her own. She felt that she had to try "at least once" to complete projects or programs on her own before seeking help. She felt that she needed to "prepare for real life." She did feel that she would still need help if she couldn't figure it out by herself, but would first try to solve problems alone.

The Calculus class, Lyn stated, was "not bad," since she felt that she had a much stronger background in this class. She stated that the teacher "really took care of everybody" and made sure that everyone understood before going on to the next step. Before any exam, she reported, he always gave them a preview of what they needed to study and what areas they needed to cover. This helped her, she stated, since she had so little time. When a teacher directed her in this way, she felt, she could be efficient. This contrasted greatly with her Computer Science class, she believed. She also stated that her Calculus teacher was "a little like a teacher from [her home country]."

Lyn's Algebra test also went well. She stated that the terminology for the course was difficult at the beginning, but after catching up with the reading, everything went well. She still felt, however, that learning the specialized terminology was difficult. She felt that the book often expected her to have too much previous knowledge, more than she actually had. She stated that once she got used to the style of writing in the textbook, however, it got easier. Once she started to "combine things, kind of figure it out, kind of combine things together," it began to make more sense. Although the definitions didn't make much sense at the beginning, the more definitions she learned and the more she could compare them to previously learned ones, the more things made sense.

The problem later in the semester was that the way that her instructors taught her courses was difficult for her to understand. Also, the way in which the textbook explained the material was hard for her to understand. Lyn stated that this style was very different from the way that she had learned mathematics before. She felt that her instructors and textbooks at The University didn't give a lot of examples to help her understand, as a textbook or a instructor in her home country would.

Lyn stated that during the fall semester she expected to have more time for study. Therefore, she planned to spend more time reading ahead. She felt that she needed "to read things right away and not fall behind." She felt now that it was necessary to "read before the class, not after the class," as she tried to do that semester. Actually, she stated, reconsidering, she needed "to do both." She stated that if she read the material before a lecture, she could understand the instructor better during lectures; if she read the material after, she could remember it better.

Lyn felt that international students should "learn the situation that they will be going into, so they are more prepared." She felt that students should be taught more about the environments that they would find themselves in. For example, she stated, in IEP writing classes, writing about general things didn't help them enough, that it "is not efficient." It was more efficient, she believed, for students to "write only in their majors." She stated that since many IEP students were unhappy about the amount of time that they had to spend in IEP classes, this would make them happier and make them feel that they were not "wasting their time." It would also help them in their future classes. This should make students happy, since "they are always looking to the future." She recognized, however, that this would be difficult for students who were new to America, since they wouldn't have any experience in their majors.

Lyn also stated that international students needed help in forming and practicing asking questions. She felt that this should be made a component of every IEP class. She also felt that the first semester in mainstream courses was difficult for an international student because they were getting used to the academic environment. Therefore, she believed, IEP courses should introduce university academic culture to the students. She stated that she realized that this would be hard because students came from so many different majors, but she believed that there were basic aspects about academic culture that could be taught. This, she believed, would help the students be more efficient in the future. She stated finally that there was a great difference between the environment of an IEP classroom and a mainstream classroom. This big difference could cause "a little culture shock," and therefore needed to be addressed.

Ayla

*"Sometimes you can feel the electric between people.
Some people have good electric, sometimes bad electric."*

The Background Interview

At the time of the study, Ayla was a twenty-four year old female graduate student from the Middle East, majoring in music. Her first language was a Middle Eastern language, which she spoke with her mother and father at home. In addition, her mother, who spent five years living and working in France, also spoke French. Her father also spoke some German, which he had studied in her home country.

Ayla first began to learn English in high school when she was fifteen years old. This high school class, she reported, which she attended for two hours each week, was strictly based on grammatical study and the memorization of vocabulary, so the class "didn't work well." It was also based, she reported, on British English. She stated, "You can't learn English from a book, but you have to use it." She felt that to learn a language, you had to use it on a daily basis and that it was extremely important to learn it naturally.

Ayla also attended college in her home country, where she worked as a graduate assistant and as "a sort of substitute teacher." While there were no English courses at her university, she did take a special course in English because she wanted to come to the United States to study and therefore had to prepare for the TOEFL test. The courses at this special school were taught by British instructors, who used tapes that "strictly taught how to pass the TOEFL test." After that course, she took the TOEFL and received a score of 450, so she felt that she needed to take the test again.

Ayla was married to an American and came to the United States in May, 1998. When first coming to America, she attended English classes at another university. She stated that she didn't like these classes as they were "mostly from the book" and were very grammar-based rather than communicative in nature.

Ayla stated that she was learning English "for her career." She felt that as a musician, wherever she went, "Japan or wherever," she would be able to use English to communicate. The business of music was "based on English," she stated, so she felt that she could use it all over the world.

Ayla stated that she used English to speak to her husband and that they spoke "basically all in English." Her husband, she reported, knew only a few words in her language like "hello" and "thank you." She stated that she liked to learn English and felt that she had a good attitude toward language learning. She considered herself a quick learner. She stated that she wanted to speak like an American, that she didn't want to "sound like a foreign person." She felt very willing to learn. She stated that she wanted to learn English for daily communication, especially with her husband, but also so that she could use it around the world. She stated that her mother had been very encouraging in this, as she had had the experience of living abroad.

As a short-term goal, Ayla first wanted "to learn correct grammar." She stated that she wanted to be able to "talk without thinking." For her long-term goal, she wanted to learn the language of music, the language of her career.

Ayla stated that she did experience culture shock when she first came to America, and again when she first began to attend The University. Much of her culture shock, she stated, was from technology. She felt that this culture shock had affected her greatly, even to the point where she had had a hard time practicing her music.

Another goal, Ayla stated, was to perfect her "presentation style." She believed that in the future, this could mean the difference between getting a job or not. In addition, she felt that she would need this better presentation style to talk to other musicians while studying her major.

Ayla's view on language learning was that students needed to study every day and needed to practice every day. They needed to be organized and practice regularly. She stated that she had many American friends at school with which to practice. She admitted, however, that she had had some trouble adapting to American school culture and daily life. She found that in America "students have no time," that "life is too busy," and that the pace of life was simply too fast.

Outside of school, Ayla liked to read magazines in English for enjoyment. She found that a magazine article could be easy to understand if she was interested in the subject. She also stated that she wrote some letters in English. She also liked to watch television, using closed captions, which she felt helped her to learn. She also did "lots of speaking" in English with her husband.

Ayla felt that reading was her "worst" subject and that academic reading was "tough." She stated that she had actually delayed taking certain music classes because of the large amount of reading involved. She felt that she needed "to understand [the readings] completely" and that she didn't "want to get a bad mark" because her reading was poor. Her writing ability, she felt, was "so-so," but felt that writing was very important, so she planned to continue to work on her writing ability. Speaking and listening, she felt, were "O.K."

Ayla stated that most activities outside of class that require English are easy to deal with. If she did have trouble, however, she stated that she would practice with her husband what to say. Speaking in her IEP classes, she felt, was easier, since her teachers and classmates were used to her. She reported that outside of class, however, "people are scared talking to me."

Ayla noted that she was not comfortable doing research. She was not comfortable with computers and technology. Typing also gave her some trouble. She stated that back in her home country, since she was in music, she never had to type. She said that she was good at taking notes and had no problem interrupting a teacher to ask a question. She believed that her vocabulary was "O.K., but not enough." She especially felt that she lacked the specialized vocabulary of her major.

The Second Interview

The second interview with Ayla took place approximately three weeks into the semester. Ayla was taking three classes at that point: Orchestra, Cello Sectional, and Dance. The Orchestra class, in which they "play pieces," was "hard right now." She stated that she was struggling to understand the musical terms. She felt that she was "not an expert," that she didn't have the background necessary to know the musical terms. In her home country, she reported, they used terms in Italian or her native language only, not in English. Here, she reported, the Orchestra leader used different terms than she was used to, terms that she had never heard before.

Ayla reported that if she didn't understand a term, she asked another person in her section of the orchestra. These people, she said, knew the terms better because they were "used to the language" and because they "have taken musical history or some other classes." She stated that other than the terms, she hadn't had any trouble understanding the instructor, who she described as "a kind, nice person."

As a graduate student, Ayla was required to play in the orchestra and had to play the most difficult pieces, such as solos. In subsequent semesters, however, she planned to drop orchestra. At that point, she felt that she had "difficult problems," which she felt she needed to solve as quickly as possible. She felt, however, that she couldn't concentrate on these problems, as she was taking too much time playing in the orchestra. She stated that she had been playing the cello for over ten years, so she "can't change overnight," that "it takes time." Therefore, she would drop the orchestra, though she planned to finish out this semester. She stated that it was not that she didn't enjoy playing in the orchestra, but rather that she had technical problems that she needed to address. She hoped to go back to the orchestra after fixing these problems. She felt that if she couldn't play well, the others in the orchestra would not accept her; therefore, she had to play well.

Ayla explained that as the principal cello, things were first explained to her by the orchestra conductor, then she was supposed to guide the others in her section. Sometimes, however, she didn't understand and had to ask members of her section for help instead, for example when she didn't know a musical term. Since she was uncomfortable with many words, she got a musical dictionary and had been writing down terms that she didn't understand, then was looking them up later to memorize. She felt, however, that she would rather get vocabulary naturally. She stated that the members of her section were not negative when she asked for help, but rather helpful, which had made the process easier.

Ayla stated that she felt "too overwhelmed and too busy right now" to go to talk to the conductor about this problem. She stated that in her home country, she was used to talking indirectly with the teacher and so was not used to talking in such a direct manner. In her home country, she stated, people were "pushed down." Teachers didn't want students to say things in a straightforward way, she claimed. While students in America were more straightforward, she believed, it would be considered rude or insubordinate in her home country. She stated that she liked the straightforward way, but was still very nervous when talking to a teacher or other person in authority that way.

Ayla believed that it was important "how you present yourself." She felt that it was fine to explain your opinion here, but that "you must be able to explain why you feel a certain way." She stated that she liked this way. In her home country, she stated, a student would "just suffer and take it." Therefore, she had been practicing with her husband how to ask direct questions and how to explain things that she didn't like.

Before going to talk to the orchestra leader, however, Ayla felt that she needed more practice first. She didn't want him to think that she blamed him, but rather that she was overwhelmed. She stated that sometimes she said things that she didn't think were bad, but "it comes out bad." She didn't like such misunderstandings. She felt that it was important that people thought well of her.

Ayla stated that her biggest problem at that point was in the Cello Sectional, since she was supposed to be the leader. In this class, the cellos, as a group, practiced what was assigned by the orchestra leader. One other person in the sectional had acted as the principal before, she stated, so sometimes he led, but mostly it was up to her to lead. She stated that "it is hard to be a leader." She felt that even in her home country, a leadership position like this would be difficult, since she was supposed to have more experience than the others and had to be able to explain things to others. However, she felt that she had problems since she had trouble "explaining things logically" and had problems using the terms at the same time. She felt that she just didn't have enough time to study those terms. She stated that she did normally like to be a leader, but in this case, she had to deal with the language, the music, and the leadership all at the same time. She stated that her sectional members had been encouraging, however. She reported that they understood her personality and didn't get upset. She felt that people in music were used to international students, which made it easier. She also stated that, when all else failed, she could always make people understand something by playing the piece on her cello and making them understand that way.

Ayla was taking the Dance class "for fun" over the lunch hour. She was taking the class only for the extra credits and for the enjoyment. She didn't want to do anything too difficult, she stated, since her other classes were difficult enough. The teacher, who was also from a non-English speaking country, made her feel comfortable, since he could understand the problems she had experienced. The other students in the class, however, were all younger students, who "have no experience with international students" and "are not used to me" and thus "had a hard time talking to me."

Ayla felt that she had to "read something over and over" to remember it. Therefore, she was trying to say the musical terms over and over again. In her Dance class, they repeated terms over and over again, so she felt that she was getting the vocabulary quickly. In orchestra, however, this didn't happen, since they were usually playing their instruments instead. In addition, there was the assumption that the students already knew the terms. Therefore, she felt that she needed to do it on her own. Ayla stated that she hadn't had any library research at this point, which made her happy since she didn't feel prepared for it.

The Third Interview

The third interview with Ayla took place immediately after spring break. During the period between the second and third interviews, Ayla had experienced a great amount of difficulty. She had experienced severe pain in her right wrist, which was initially thought to be carpal tunnel syndrome. At the time of the interview, her wrist was getting better, however. The doctors had discovered that it was tendonitis, not carpal tunnel syndrome. She was required by the doctors to rest her hand and wear a brace. In addition, she was receiving therapy three times a week.

Because of the injury to her wrist, Ayla was no longer playing the cello. Instead, she went to Orchestra and Cello Sectional to observe and occasionally gave recommendations. She was the leader of the Cello Sectional, so some leadership was still expected of her. She was still trying to contribute, since it was part of her assistantship to be the principal.

Ayla stated that it was still not easy to give suggestions or directions, but felt that at that point she could give better recommendations, since she was able to sit back and view the whole situation more easily. She stated that her department had been very supportive, as had the orchestra leader, who had been having her look at the orchestra parts and the sheet music along with him as the orchestra played. Sometimes he asked her questions about what she was thinking. She found it very interesting to look at the orchestra as a whole, something that she was normally not able to do. This had enabled her to see how the conductor read the parts as well. She stated that this was difficult to understand, seeing all the parts at once. She felt that it would take her a long time to be able to see the entire orchestra playing at once. She was enjoying getting this extra experience, however, and was enjoying learning things that she would normally never be able to learn.

Right now, Ayla felt that these experiences had been good for her. She felt that she "tried to do too much at the beginning" and "tried to force myself too much." When she first came to The University, she stated, her first impression was that everyone was working hard. So she thought, "O.K., let's do it." She felt that she was always a hard worker, but not as hard a worker as she became at the beginning of the semester. It turned out to be too much for her, she now believed. She stated that she was working hard with her muscles, not just mentally hard. Additionally, she was doing the same actions over and over again. She stated that subsequently, she was not going to do that anymore. Therefore, she felt that this whole experience had been good for her, since she was now able to concentrate more on learning English, while still learning something about the orchestra. She felt that it had helped her change her attitude.

Ayla felt that she was now able to take some time to relax and think through what she needed to do in the following semesters. She found that it was much easier to think things through at that point. She stated that she now understood better what she was supposed to do, rather than "killing" herself.

Ayla's plan at that point was to try to take more English classes instead of music, then go back to music afterwards. At that point, she stated, she could understand her music classes, but wanted to understand better. She wanted to get better marks, though that was not what was important. "What is important," she believed, "is to understand."

This need to understand was important, Ayla stated, because her friends in her major had told her that she had to read many papers in music history and music theory classes. As they had said, she "had to read and keep reading." Right now, she stated, she could read fairly well, but she wanted to understand more of what she read. She wanted to be able to concentrate on the concepts and issues and not have to concentrate so much on the individual words. She stated that in the near future, she would be taking a compact class, which covered material much faster, so she would therefore have an even harder time. She would have to read many essays and research papers, she reported.

Ayla stated that she hoped to soon take an IEP reading class, writing class, and grammar class, since she felt that all three components came together to help her. She felt happy to be able to do this for now, since it would give her a chance to relax her wrist and to concentrate on English. She stated that it was now easier to think, that her "brain was coming apart." She felt that she could now focus on what she had to do, and not put too much pressure on herself.

Ayla reported that her experiences with her wrist had also made her rethink her future. She stated that after finishing her music major, she planned to switch to a different major. She stated that she wanted another career to fall back on if she couldn't get a job in music. While she would definitely do a different major, however, she was committed to finishing her music degree.

Ayla stated that she felt she needed to take a class in learning how to speak or present in front of a group. She felt that public presentation was very important. She stated that she "needs to be able to reach people, or they won't listen." She stated that this was a "human thing, not a language thing." Even in one's own language, she felt, it was difficult, though extremely important, to know how to present oneself.

Ayla felt, therefore, that the IEP should have had more chances to practice presentations. She also believed that the IEP should tell both "how and why" to say things. They should not just teach "how to say things, don't just focus on the

English. That is the easy part." Instead, she believed students "need the reasons why you say something . . . Every one is going through culture shock, so everyone needs it."

Ayla also stated that she felt that much of her daily interaction was with other international students, not Americans. She felt that more should be done to get international students to interact with Americans. This, she felt, would help international students understand better and make their life easier, not just in the classroom, but in daily life as well. She felt that if a student was comfortable in their daily life, they could focus better on their classroom life. "It will make them more confident," she added.

In retrospect, Ayla wished that she had not "killed myself at the beginning of the semester." She felt that she should have started reading textbooks much earlier, because of the large amount of reading at the beginning of the semester. She felt that she was not a patient person and got frustrated from reading. Therefore, if she had started earlier, she felt, she would have been less frustrated.

Ayla felt that while she had not accomplished what she wanted in her classes, she had achieved something psychologically. "Things are getting better now," she stated, which improved her outlook. She now felt confident about concentrating on learning English.

The Class Observation

The observation for Ayla took place during a Cello Sectional practice session. This observation took place in one of the practice rooms in the Music Building. It was a sparse room, with only sound dampers on the walls and no windows. The only things in the room were chairs, music holders, and a piano in one corner.

While the group practiced, Ayla sat slightly off to the side, where the others could see her only if they turned. She was ostensibly in charge and suggested that they get started. She was not very assertive in her leadership, however. This was marked by not sitting in front where they could see her.

The majority of the class was filled with the playing of music. The group only practiced one selection the entire hour. The first time they played it through from start to finish. One member then made a suggestion that they start at a certain point because he stated that he was having trouble at that spot. When they played that section, he stopped the group and asked a question. Ayla and one other member made suggestions, with the other demonstrating on her cello what she meant. Ayla seemed to agree.

When Ayla made her suggestion, it did not seem to have any of the problems that she had discussed with me in previous interviews. The others seemed to understand her suggestion quite easily and to take her suggestion well. She remained unobtrusive.

When the class session was finished, no one explicitly stated that they were through. They all just packed up their instruments and left. They all seemed to function well as a unit without anyone really being the leader.

The Fourth Interview

Ayla stated that she was now getting used to talking in the Cello Sectional. "They know me and I know them," she stated. She had told them that she was still learning English, so they didn't get upset with her when she said something incorrectly. She told them to "just be patient." She stated that they were nice people and that she liked them. She found that the more she got to know them, the easier things were. She stated, "Relationship is everything." She continued by saying that "sometimes you can feel the electric between people. Some people have good electric, sometimes bad electric." She stated that she had chosen to be with the Cello Sectional, so there was "good electric" between them. She felt that if she had "bad electric" with someone, she didn't want to be friends with them. She also felt that it made a big difference in the group if the members "feel natural." Many groups are "fake," she stated, but this one was "natural." She knew them well and felt that "they are nice people."

She was finding it easier now to give criticism or suggestions. She stated that it was easier because she now knew the members of her group so well. In addition, she was getting more comfortable with speaking English, so that helped to make it easier as well. Also, she had been getting more knowledge about the cello, which made it both easier and faster for her to give criticism or suggestions.

Ayla stated that she didn't feel like she had to be the leader of this group for the group to be successful. They were all "mature students," she believed, and they did better when they were "more like a team, with everyone helping each other instead of one leader."

Ayla also stated that by sitting back and observing, she felt that she was learning more about the cello and "how to speak the language of music," because she could observe the others and how they acted without the pressure or distraction of playing her cello. She stated that once again, the experience had been good for her.

The Final Interview

The final interview with Ayla took place after the end of the semester. Because of the injury to her wrist, Ayla was not able to play the cello for the remainder of the semester. Therefore, in spite of attending classes and giving advice to the other members of her section, she reported that she had to take an incomplete for the Cello Sectional class. However, the instructor had given her the chance to get her two credits for the class. She needed to create five lesson plans in place of playing the cello. He had given her one year to complete this assignment; however, she stated that she planned to complete the assignment over the summer.

Since the Orchestra was part of her assistantship, and not for a grade, Ayla had technically completed her obligation by her attendance at each session. She believed that she had learned more about the orchestra from observing it than she had from playing in it by virtue of following along with the conductor's score. She stated that she found the experience very enlightening. As stated earlier, she had dropped her Dance class.

Ayla stated that, since she did not feel very secure in her major, she wanted to get her degree as soon as possible, then begin studying a different major. She didn't feel secure in the United States with a degree in music. She felt that if she were planning to go back to her home country, she would be more confident in the major. Since she was staying in America, however, she felt that she needed a second major to fall back on.

Ayla reported that she would be taking "three very difficult classes" during the upcoming semester. She felt that she had to approach these classes in a different way. She stated that she "must fight in these classes." She felt that she had to work especially hard during the first part of the semester. She felt that the work would be difficult at the beginning, but she had to "be patient during the beginning," then "everything will get better later." She planned to also familiarize herself with research at the beginning of the semester, since it would begin to play a heavy role in her classes. She reiterated that she needed "to fight hard at the beginning of the semester."

Ayla also stated that she planned to ask the teacher for additional help, if possible, as well as to ask for help from her friends in the program. She also stated that she wanted to get ahead of the reading and do as much reading as possible at the beginning of the semester. She stated that she would "try to find the main points through skimming and scaning, like [her IEP reading teacher] taught me." She stated that she couldn't read everything assigned, that "it isn't possible." Instead, she had to figure out the main points and ideas and "what the author wants to make us understand." She reiterated that it was impossible to read everything. "It is like reading a newspaper," she explained. You don't want to read every word. Instead, "you look at the headlines and see if that story interests you. If not, you don't read that story."

Ayla stated that she felt that since most IEP students go on to take classes in their major, they "need recommendations with those classes." Therefore, she believed that it would be helpful if the IEP could provide continued help with those classes, perhaps looking over the papers and homework required for the classes. She would like to see a more formal system of helping students out with their mainstream classes. She felt that it made her more confident if she knew that "someone is around to help." She stated that she felt she needed her IEP teachers' help not just in IEP classes, but after the classes as well. If she had the help and support of the teachers in the IEP, she claimed, she felt more confident outside, which made a big difference in her daily life, both in classes and "on the street." She stated that once students had learned the system, they would be fine. Learning the system was the hard part, she believed, that students had to "fight hard to get through the beginning," but with the help of IEP teachers, that fight could be won.

CHAPTER FIVE
DISCUSSION OF THE FINDINGS

Introduction

This chapter will offer discussion of the findings from the six informants in this study set within the framework of the research questions posed.

The Research Questions

1. What variables in the background of the informants were the most helpful in making the transition?

An important variable in the background of the informants that was very helpful in making the transition was to have previous experience with or exposure to the content of the courses that informants were taking. This seemed to be especially important in the area of exposure to the vocabulary of the content material, supporting Saville-Troike's (1984) supposition that "vocabulary knowledge in English is the most important aspect of English proficiency for academic achievement" (p. 216).

It became apparent throughout the study that this previous exposure could be gained either formally or informally. One example of how previous formal study was beneficial comes from Mari. Her past experiences with microcomputers came from actually having taken a similar course in her home country. In this course, she felt that she was relearning information that she had acquired previously, which helped to reinforce that previous learning. In this way, she believed, it was "kind of a review" for her and she was able to "learn again," this time in English, however. Similarly, Romulo had taken several previous courses in graphics and thus, like Mari, was able to directly transfer previously learned concepts and vocabulary to the new course. This was beneficial to Romulo because he was able to focus on learning to use the required computer software programs, rather than being forced to focus on learning the concepts of computer graphics or the associated vocabulary. For Lyn, even having taken a Calculus class in high school fifteen years previously proved to be beneficial in that it made her more confident toward the material covered.

This previous knowledge did not have to come from formal study to prove helpful, however. Informal exposure also proved to be beneficial. For Romulo, for example, familiarity with public relations learned on the job in his home country gave him an edge, he felt, over his less experienced classmates. Even less formally, Romulo was familiar with the vocabulary and concepts of astronomy from watching television programs and from reading magazines. For Samory, experience and familiarity with the concepts and vocabulary of "sustainable development," an area covered in his Environmental Economics class, came from informally reading books on the subject, some of which he had read on his own, and one of which he had read for his IEP reading class. For Samory, this background knowledge was important because it made it possible for him to ask questions about the subject in class, which he felt was the best way for him to learn.

On the other hand, it is important to note that familiarity and experience with a subject did not always prove to be beneficial. In the case of Mari, who had previously taken a history course similar to the one that she took at The University, her history class at The University was taught in a very different style from the course she had taken in her home country, with a very different underlying philosophy about the teaching of history. This style asked her not only to memorize names and dates, but to interpret history as well. Because the course style did not meet her expectations, it proved a difficult obstacle for her, in spite of her previously learned knowledge. Similarly, Lyn had taken many mathematics courses in the past, but they had been taught in a different style and with a different underlying philosophy, which asked her not only to memorize formulas, but to understand the underlying theory behind the formulas as well. These findings support the work of Gradman and Hanania (1991) who found that teachers' styles correlated with academic success of international students.

A further variable that proved to be helpful for many of the informants, especially in the initial stages of the semester, was the support of others. This support took many forms among the informants. For Samory, support came initially from fellow students from his home country who had been studying at The University for a longer period than he. This was especially helpful to Samory since the others from his home country were in the same program and had previously taken many of the classes that he was taking and could therefore give him guidance and advice. Samory's experience certainly supports the contention made by Clarke (1994), who includes establishing "native language support groups for use in and outside class" in his list of potential "instructional initiatives" for educational change (p. 5).

Support from family members also proved to be important. For Romulo, that support came mainly from his wife. In addition to practicing English with her and "correcting each other," Romulo was able to have his wife examine his written work and to discuss his courses, especially his history course, since his wife had taken several history courses previously and was thus more knowledgeable about the subject. Similarly, Fernanda had the support of her brother, who had been living in the United States for over ten years and who had himself previously studied at The University. Therefore, Fernanda had someone to turn to for advice and guidance regarding life in the United States and study at The University. Lyn and Ayla were also able to received guidance and advice from their husbands, both of whom had studied at other American universities. The experience of these informants supports Wilhelm (1995), who found that the number of family members who had studied in English-speaking countries was one of nine language learning background variables most closely associated with success in an intensive English program.

Support from others also came from other international students, many of whom the informants knew from their time in the IEP. As Harklau (1994) found in her study of a U.S. high school, ESL classes can play "a facilitative role in the formation of peer networks and adjustments to U.S. school and society" (p. 265). She found that the ESL program was "instrumental in the development of peer relationships among immigrants from various linguistic and cultural backgrounds at the school" (p. 265). Such support provided the informants in this study with a connection to, and information from, students outside their own ethnic or language backgrounds, thus widening their support base.

Another variable in the background of informants that proved to be helpful was previous exposure to American culture. For Samory, this exposure came from his previous experience working with Americans in one of his jobs back in his home country. This was especially helpful to him when doing writing projects. He considered writing to be his strongest ability, since he felt that his experiences of writing on the job had given him a good understanding of the "American style." For Lyn, her exposure came from having lived in the United States for a long period of time. This allowed her to be very comfortable with her daily life, which in turn allowed her to be better able to concentrate on her courses. It was also helpful in that she felt that it was no longer embarrassing to her if someone didn't understand her, as she felt it would be to someone new to the country.

Keeping a positive attitude about courses and university life also proved to be beneficial. As Stern (1975) writes, "Good learners can often adapt to almost any learning condition" (p. 311). Samory, for example, believed that he could not change his situation and could not expect his instructors to change their style to fit him. Therefore, he believed that it was his job to change to match his instructors' styles. This provides support for Stern's assertion that "the good learner actively initiates the learning process and throughout adopts an attitude of personal responsibility for his own learning" (p. 312). A further example comes from Ayla who, when having difficulties with her wrist, chose to look at the situation positively and to use the time to her benefit by studying English. Because of their attitudes, both informants were able to reach past difficulties and remain productive. Additionally, Ayla saw herself as a leader. This was helpful to her since she was expected to give leadership and direction to her sectional members in the orchestra. Because of her positive self perception, she was able to provide this leadership in spite of the feeling of being at a linguistic loss at times.

2. What variables in the background of the informants caused the most difficulties in making the transition?

In contrast to the discussion above, lack of exposure to, or lack of experience with, a particular subject had a perceptible detrimental effect, especially in the area of vocabulary. The most obvious example of this was the difficulty that Samory experienced in his Soil Resources class. In this course, Samory felt that he had absolutely no background in the subject, had never studied anything related to the subject, and therefore the vocabulary of the subject was entirely new to him. This was particularly problematic, in Samory's view, because he felt that his classmates did have the necessary background knowledge to understand. Therefore, the instructor had to teach to the higher level of the class as a whole, not down to the level that Samory perceived himself to be at, putting him at a disadvantage. This is similar to Harklau's (1994) finding, in her study of language minority students placed in mainstream, English-medium classrooms in a U.S. high school, that "curriculum in subject areas depended on continuity, with content in any one course built upon a knowledge base that students were assumed to possess from previous courses in the sequence" (p. 257). Because of this perceived knowledge deficit, Samory felt that he spent the entire semester simply trying to catch up with the background knowledge of the rest of the students in his class. Further, Samory felt that this lack of knowledge left him unable to know what questions to ask in class. This caused him great concern because he felt that asking questions was the best way for him to learn. This lack of background knowledge was also problematic for Ayla. In her case, as a music major, she had studied music for many years in her home country. However, she had studied music and musical terms in her native language and in Italian only, but had never studied it in English, and therefore had a great deal of trouble using musical terms.

Conversely, previous exposure to a subject could also get in the way of learning, as in the case of Romulo and his Computer Graphics class. Terminology was a problem for Romulo in this class because, while many of the terms used in the class were familiar to him from his previous exposure to the field, the terms were used differently in his native language than they were in English. Therefore, Romulo felt that his previous knowledge of the terms was actually holding him back in learning the concepts covered in the class, reporting that it took him until the end of the semester to get fully comfortable with the terms as they were used in this situation.

Lack of experience and knowledge about conducting library research was also a common theme among the informants. Part of this problem was the perceived large size of the library. Many of the informants perceived the library to be much bigger than the libraries that they were accustomed to in their home countries, believing that there was simply too much material to sort through while doing research. They found that the process of finding a source, reading it, then evaluating its usefulness was very time consuming. In their home countries, many of the informants reported, access to the actual stacks of books would have been limited or their instructors would have been more prescriptive regarding what sources to use. Additionally, some informants had simply never done any library research at all in the past. Ayla, for example, as a music major in her home country, had never been expected to do library research.

Another aspect of this problem with research was the perceived difficulty of using the library's computer system. Ayla, for example, because she had never had to do any library research, felt very anxious about using "computers and technology." Informants felt that using the library's computer system was also time consuming, taking a long time to complete the steps required to find sources, which in turn made it difficult to decide if the sources were actually useful or not.

The students' research tasks themselves were also thought of as problematic. Part of the problem was the broad nature of the research questions that informants were given, as well as the problem of deciding how to get started doing research. Mari, for example, found research difficult because of the abstract nature of what she was reading, which made it difficult for her to understand how to begin her research. Romulo felt that the subjects his instructors gave him were too broad, forcing him to look at too wide a variety of materials. For Fernanda, lack of background knowledge played a part in her difficulties with research. Because she felt unsure about her topic, she had a hard time evaluating the usefulness of her sources. The above discussion supports the findings of Leki and Carson (1994), whose study of former ESL students currently enrolled in content courses showed that "management strategies," which include how to use the library, how to gather materials, and how to decide which sources would be appropriate for a given topic, figured prominently in student success. A large number of their respondents indicated that they "would have liked their [intensive English program] classes to prepare them, or to prepare them better, for writing which required finding, selecting, and synthesizing sources" (p. 92). They report on one student who felt that his greatest problem was "how to pick information for others [sic] courses and use it effectively as illustrations in my paper. Such sources include any outside information other than the required text. In another word [sic], how to research, and which or what kind of material is appropriate to use and which are not" (p. 92).

Anxiety about technology was not limited to doing library research, however. Several of the informants expressed a fear of technology in general, and computers in specific, mostly because they had had little or no experiences using computers in their home country. Additionally, some informants felt that even though they had experience using computers, this experience was gathered in an informal setting and that therefore they were unsure of the proper terminology of using a computer. Even if they knew the functions, they felt, they wouldn't know how to talk about and effectively express to their instructors what they had done on the computer. This anxiety about technology was the most acute for Fernanda, since her major was heavily dependent on technology. Because she had entered her program at midyear, she felt that she was behind the others in her program in regards to technology. This in turn, because of the competition that she felt existed in her program, put her at a distinct disadvantage in regards to the others in her program, she believed.

A further variable in the background of the informants that caused them difficulty was the lack of exposure to certain types of tests. This supports the results of Smoke's (1988) survey of ESL students who had completed developmental writing classes. Smoke found that 71 percent of the students in the survey reported having problems answering exam questions. For Samory, for example, this lack of experience was with multiple choice tests. Because of his lack of experience, having never taken such types of tests previously, he misjudged how much time the test would take and ran out of time at the end. He was also unaccustomed to the pressure placed on a student in such a test style and to studying for tests that required rote memorization, which led to anxiety on his part. Therefore, he had a difficult time studying for and taking that type of test, and felt, as did the students in Horwitz, Horwitz, & Cope, (1986) who reported "freezing" on tests. They had learned the material but felt that their performance on tests did not reflect their true level of knowledge.

For Fernanda, on the other hand, difficulty arose when taking essay tests. While she was used to taking multiple choice exams, she was not accustomed to taking essay exams. Because of her lack of experience, she had a difficult time deciding what and how to study for her tests and was left unable to answer all of the essay questions on her tests. Both Samory and Fernanda reported doing well on all homework assignments and doing well on the parts of tests that they were accustomed to, but ended up having their grade reduced because of doing poorly on one section of the test.

Also a factor in the transition for many students was the lack of experience with certain types of text styles. This supports the findings of Shuck's (1995) survey of students' perceptions of how IEP courses prepared them for university courses. Shuck found that students needed to be introduced to a wider variety of genres of writing, especially undergraduates who wanted "more readings of any type" (p. 44). This was especially true for both Mari and Romulo, who were both undergraduates. While they had become accustomed to reading textbooks, they were also expected, in addition to their textbooks, to read historical novels, historical narratives, and poetry books which were styles of writing that they were not accustomed to. Particularly problematic with these books was that they assumed a previous knowledge of history that neither of the informants possessed. Of particular difficulty for Romulo were the type of assignments associated with these different types of texts. In his History of Western Civilization course, he was not only expected to read historical novels and historical narratives, but also to write creatively about them, as if he were a reporter from the time period being studied. This was a difficult assignment for him to complete, since he had never been required to do such a task in the past, either in English or his native language.

Related to this was the fact that the informants were unaccustomed to certain instructional contexts and instructors' expectations. Ostler (1980) found that 34 percent of the respondents to her academic needs survey expressed a need to be able to write lab reports. For Samory, a lack of experience doing laboratory assignments caused difficulty while he was in the laboratory environment for his Soil Resources class. While he was able to follow the directions and complete the lab work, he had a difficult time making the interpretations that were required of him, never having had to do such work in his previous school experiences. Leki and Carson (1994) found that 14 percent of the responses regarding difficulties in content classes had to do with critical thinking skills - the ability to think critically and analytically, and not just memorize information. For Lyn, such difficulty emerged from her instructor's different philosophy about learning mathematics. In her home country, she was only expected to memorize formulas and to repeat those formulas on her tests. In her math class at The University, however, she had to understand the theory behind the formulas as well, something that she had never been expected to know previously.

Also problematic for the informants were expectations of how to interact with their instructors. For Fernanda, the problem was that she felt that instructors and students were considered to be at different levels in American classrooms, with the instructor above the student, while in her home country, in her opinion, they would have been considered equals. For Ayla, problems arose from the fact that she was not accustomed to talking directly to her instructors, since in her home country she would have been expected to speak indirectly to them. In her home country, she would always talk to her instructors in an indirect manner. If she had a problem she would be expected to "just live with the problem." In America, however, she was aware that she could not simply sit back and say nothing when she had a problem and that she would be expected to talk directly to her instructors about the problems that she was having. However, because of her inexperience with this style, talking directly to her instructors proved difficult.

A further problem for both Mari and Lyn was difficulty in asking questions. Stern (1975) writes, "The good language learner is not afraid, tense, or "up-tight" about the new language. He approaches it with an open and relaxed attitude" (p. 312). This proved difficult for Mari, however, since she lacked confidence in asking questions and was highly intimidated by the large size of her classes. She felt that she would be holding her classmates back by asking questions and would interrupt the flow of the class and would therefore remain silent, even if it meant not understanding the instructor's lecture. She also felt intimidated toward asking questions if she felt that she wouldn't be able to articulate her question exactly, supporting Horowitz, etal, (1996) who write, "We note that a number of students believe nothing should be said in the foreign language until it can be said correctly and that it is not okay to guess an unknown foreign word" (p. 127).

Lyn, on the other hand, while not being afraid or embarrassed to ask questions in front of classmates, found difficulty in knowing how to construct questions, reporting that by the time she had mentally constructed the question, the instructor would already have progressed to the next topic and her chance was missed.

Lyn also felt held back by the fact that it had been a number of years since she had studied at college; she felt that she was out of practice at reading and studying, and was therefore "a slow reader," which would ultimately hold her back.

Mari expressed difficulty in reading and responding to the business letters that she wrote for her Business Correspondence course. While she could understand the words and grammar of the written correspondence, she had difficulty understanding the underlying cultural meanings, which affected her performance on quizzes and tests, since she had a difficult time imagining the situations that she was reading about, and therefore had a difficult time responding to them.

3. Do undergraduate and graduate students go through similar or different processes as they make the transition?

One of the greatest differences between the experiences of undergraduates and graduate students was the size of the classes that they participated in. While graduate students had relatively small class sizes, undergraduates had much larger class sizes to contend with, where the vast majority of students were native English speakers. These greater class sizes caused distractions, making it more difficult for informants to hear and understand their instructors. Harklau (1994) found that ESL students, because they were not explicitly required to participate in classroom interactions given the large number of students vying for the floor in content classes, would tune out many mainstream instructional interactions entirely. The students paid little attention to their teachers or peers, instead depending as Mari did, on "just going home and studying more." Harklau explains this as "partially a function of input that students found incomprehensible, and partially a function of their preferences for interaction with written materials. The net result was that students were often withdrawn and non-interactive in mainstream classes. They were not even paying particular attention to the input, much less engaging in interaction" (p. 252). The experiences of the undergraduates in the study certainly support the contention of Lucas and Wagner (1999), who include the prescription, "Place transitioning students in smaller classes so they can get more personal attention" in their list of "Strategies for Facilitating the Transition" of language learners into the mainstream (p. 9).

Ostler (1980) found that 68 percent of her informants reported the need to ask questions in class. However, large classes also made it very difficult for some of the informants, such as Mari, to ask questions in class, since they were intimidated by large audiences. This supports the conclusions of Harklau (1994), who found in her study that:

> Classes of up to 35 students were large and unwieldy to facilitate interactions, and the demands that teachers faced to cover the material often made classroom discussion a luxury. As a result, teacher-led discussions featuring the familiar initiation-reply-evaluation (IRE)

> sequence (Mehan 1979) were the prevalent mode of instruction. In an average class, all other things being equal, individual students only had a 1:25 or 1:30 chance of being allocated a turn by the teacher during these activities. (p. 250)

If we believe, along with Johnson (1983) and Strong (1983) that the degree of active participation in communication with English-speaking peers is a significant factor in second language learning, these students were not getting the communicative practice they needed to develop as second language speakers. This problem was made even greater by the intimidation factor.

Graduate students, however, given their relatively small classes and the fact that the same students were in each class, were able to form closer relationships with their classmates. This helped in several different ways. Samory, for example, as he was able to get to know his classmates better and become more comfortable with them, was able to study with them and practice for tests together, as well as to practice the ability to more easily produce the questions that he wanted to ask in class. This was important for Samory because this was the way that he felt was the best method for him to learn. Similarly, Ayla was able to form a close relationship with her fellow Cello Sectional members, which helped her not only perform the leadership duties that were required of her, but also to give her the emotional support she needed when she hurt her wrist. Smaller classes also helped Romulo, a more advanced undergraduate, in that it helped him form closer relationships with classmates, which in turn helped him overcome his perception that Americans were "closed-minded."

Another large difference between the experiences of undergraduate students and graduate students was the types of classes that they were taking. Gradman and Hanania (1991) found that successful students were those who perceived that what they were learning would be useful to them in the future, while negative reactions were elicited from those who felt that it was not useful when courses were imposed on them. In the case of undergraduates, they were required to meet credit requirements by taking classes that weren't in their major field. This caused a problem in that the undergraduates felt that they were learning things that would not be useful to them in the future and that they were therefore wasting their time. As Shuck (1995) has written, "University students - particularly those from other countries - tend to be very pragmatic. They are understandably concerned about what will help them the most right now" (p. 45). This was especially acute for Romulo, who felt that he would never use the knowledge that he was gaining in either History of Western Civilization or Astronomy in the future. While he felt the classes would not be useful, to pass the course he did need to learn the associated vocabulary and study for the tests, which was difficult and time consuming, taking away time and energy from the courses that he thought would be useful to him in the future. For both Romulo and Mari this was a great problem because they were both already extremely busy and these classes took precious time away from the classes that they did think would be useful in the future.

Further, for Mari, because of the wide choice of possible courses that she was given, she ended up taking courses that were not what she initially expected. She originally thought, for example, that her History class would be about American history, which it was not. Additionally, she thought that her Volleyball course would simply require playing volleyball, but instead involved learning how to teach volleyball and was not what she had expected. Because the courses did not match her expectations and took a greater amount of her time, her motivation toward these classes was decreased.

Conversely, graduate students were much more limited in the types of courses that were available to them in their programs and their courses were much more prescribed. While the undergraduates in the study had too wide a variety of courses, as a graduate student who had very specific goals in mind, Samory believed that his choice of courses was too limited, in that the exact courses he was interested in were not available on any given semester and that he felt that he was taking classes that were not directly related to what he wanted to do in the future. Without a direct correlation to future use, he felt a lack of motivation for learning the material.

For Fernanda, problems arose in that her classes were sequenced. Because she entered her program in the middle of the school year, she was not able to take the first courses in the sequence. While the other students in her program had taken the courses before, she lacked the knowledge that the others had gained in the previous courses in the sequence, which she felt put her at a disadvantage, especially in the environment of competition that she perceived as being prevalent in her department.

A positive difference, on the side of undergraduates, was that they had a wider array of formal support structures to help them successfully complete their courses. As Stern (1975) has written, "[The good language learner] seizes every opportunity to practice and use the language and actively co-operates with his teacher by responding to the opportunities for practice provided" (p. 314). Both Mari and Romulo followed this maxim and took advantage of the opportunities given them. They both had the opportunity to attend formal study sessions for their History of Western Civilization courses. And while the Learning Center was open to both undergraduate and graduate students, the program is definitely designed for undergraduates, with tutors that specialize in different undergraduate subjects.

Conversely, however, Ayla, as a graduate student, was expected to take a much greater leadership role in her program of study and was required not only, as a graduate assistant, to play her instrument, but to lead the Cello Sectional as well, which put added strain on her already stressful study.

4. What variables encountered in the environment were the most helpful in making the transition?

One helpful variable encountered in the environment was the fact that several of the informants were able to do hands-on work, especially work in labs or while sitting at computer terminals. This had the benefit that it fit the learning styles of several of the informants, who could both learn and practice what they were learning at the same time. By being able to have a process modeled for them directly and then being able to practice that process directly after on a computer, informants were able to learn in a better, more efficient way.

Skilton & Meyer (1993) found that "while all of the teachers and 91% of the students surveyed agreed that students should ask more questions in class, in terms of behavior, students did not ask questions in class" (p. 89). In many ways, working directly on a computer had added benefits in this area. First, it allowed the informants to be able to ask the instructor questions about their work directly. Pica & Doughty (1985) found that the participation structure influenced interaction, that students in small groups and one-to-one interaction with the instructor interacted more than they did in teacher-fronted classrooms. In the teacher-fronted activities, students asked far fewer questions than during small-group work. They write, "18.6% of student questions were asked during teacher-fronted activities as opposed to 81.4% during small-group activities" (p. 90). More comprehension and clarification checks were also asked during large class discussions, while more turn-taking and language production took place during small group activities. Such opportunities away from teacher-centered activities were especially helpful for Mari, who had trouble asking questions in front of large groups. By working directly on a computer, she was able to ask questions in such a way that she would not feel embarrassed. The types of questions asked also differed greatly in these situations. Pica & Doughty (1985) write that they "found overall that students asked far more open referential questions, confirmation checks and clarification requests during small-group activities than during teacher-fronted activities" (p. 91). This was important for Lyn, who had difficulty forming the questions that she wanted to ask in a way that would get her point across effectively. She was able to ask effective questions to a much greater degree when she could point directly to the material on a computer screen.

A variable that further helped the informants in the study was that with time in their individual classes and programs, they began to adapt better. Christison & Krahnke (1986) write, "Many subjects mentioned an initial difficulty in comprehending lectures, but most said that their skills increased rapidly with real experience" (p. 73). It was apparent in this study that as informants became more accustomed to such things as teachers' styles, presentation styles, test types, and especially to their teachers' voices, they began to better understand what was expected of them and how to perform better in those classes. This seemed to happen for all of the informants in the study near the middle of the semester.

Also valuable for informants was that with time, they began to know the people in their programs better, which helped them adapt better. Romulo, for example, initially felt that people at The University were "closed-minded." However, when he got to know people in his major classes, he began to change his mind. Once again, for virtually all of the informants in the study, this change in perception began to occur around the middle of the semester. For Ayla, getting to know her fellow Cello Sectional members better proved valuable in that they were able to give her support when her wrist became hurt.

For Samory, of great help was the fact that he had previous experience working with Americans, and was therefore familiar with the American style of writing. Therefore, when he wrote things for his classes, he found that his style of writing matched his previous exposure and was successful in his writing assignments.

For Ayla, a further variable encountered that helped her succeed was the fact that her department was willing to give the extra time and extra help that she needed while recovering from her wrist injury. She was able to continue to contribute to the orchestra, in spite of not being able to play her instrument, by participating with the orchestra leader, as well as being allowed to write lesson plans to make up for the fact that she could not play in her Cello Sectional.

5. What variables encountered in the environment caused the most difficulties in making the transition?

For all of the informants in the study, the variable that affected them the most was the lack of time to complete all of the work that was required of them. Because of the large amount of reading and homework that was required of the informants, they had a hard time completing all tasks, which in turn made it difficult to find time to study for tests or complete projects. This problem was exacerbated in that informants did not begin reading their assigned materials at the start of the semester, which then forced them to spend the rest of the semester trying to catch up with reading and work. Informants also were not prepared for the large amount of outside class activities that they were required to participate in, including group work.

Ostler (1980) found that 90 percent of respondents in her survey reported needing to read textbooks, making it obviously one of the most important skills needed. What this number does not reflect, however, is the large *amount* of materials that university students have to read. Directly related to this was the large amount of materials that they had to read at any one given time. Several informants commented that the required readings were not that difficult, but rather that the problem lay in the large amount of reading that they had to complete in a short period of time. Several informants fell behind during the initial stages of the semester and then had to spend the remainder of the semester trying to catch up with the reading, which put a time strain on finishing projects and studying for tests. For Romulo and Mari, this burden was made greater by the large number of names and dates that they were required to memorize for their history classes.

As Freiermuth (2001) points out (citing cf. Goffman, 1974), "The frame of what constitutes effective group interaction and task resolution is not consistent across cultures" (p. 172). Therefore, a further variable that had a profound effect on the informants was the amount of, and difficulty in doing, group work. This group work came in many, varied forms. For Samory, the group work took place in a laboratory class. There he felt that it was difficult for him to share his work with others, since he had never been required to do such group work previously. For Mari, group work was difficult because she found it intimidating to speak in front of groups of people and had an especially difficult time expressing her opinion in such situations, especially when she was expected to develop her opinion quickly. She felt that in these situations she was not expressing her true opinion, since she was accustomed to being able to take as much time as needed to formulate an opinion. Both Romulo and Fernanda expressed cultural difficulties in working with Americans in groups and expressed the belief that group work functioned differently in their own cultures. Fernanda had the most difficult time with this, experiencing problems with the hierarchical nature of group work in her program, as well as the spirit of competition among the groups, something that she was unaccustomed to.

Closely related to the problems that informants experienced with group work was difficulty in giving presentations, which also came in many different forms. While Ostler (1980) found that graduate students had a greater level of need for this skill, this study found that both undergraduates and graduates needed this skill to a great degree. Once again, Mari had difficulties because she felt intimidated expressing her opinion in front of groups, especially when she was expected to develop her opinion quickly. For Fernanda, difficulties arose from the fact that she was required to give very formal presentations, but had never had prior opportunities to find out what a formal presentation should look like, and thus was at a loss. She also felt unsure about her topics, worrying that her classmates, who had entered the program a semester before her, would be more knowledgeable about the subject than she and thus would ask her questions that she would not be able to answer.

For virtually all of the informants in the study, conducting research also caused difficulties. In her survey, Smoke (1988) found that 56 percent of the informants "felt nervous" when a research paper was required for a class, and a full 37 percent "revealed that they would drop the course" if a research paper was required (p. 13). As noted earlier, informants in this study found the size of the library and the library's computer system to be intimidating, with the library being much bigger than the libraries that they were used to in their home countries and that there was simply too much material to sort through while doing research. Finding a source, reading it, then evaluating it was simply too time consuming, given other time constraints. Informants were also anxious about using the technology involved with library research, since they had never used such systems in their home countries. Several of the informants also expressed difficulties with assignments that were perceived as being too broad or too abstract, and expressed difficulty in knowing how to get started doing research and being forced to look at too wide a range of materials. This lack of understanding of the topic contributed to the problem of not being able to effectively evaluate sources.

Note taking also posed a problem for the informants, supporting the conclusions of Smoke (1988), who found that 74 percent of the students in her survey reported having difficulty "taking notes from a lecture class" (p. 13). If the informants concentrated too hard on individual words, they would loose track of the main ideas of the lecture and miss the overall meaning. This was a large problem for Mari, who spent a great amount of time looking up words in her dictionary. For Mari and Romulo, taking notes on names and dates from history proved especially problematic. Specialized words and acronyms also posed a problem for Fernanda, since she was unaccustomed to such things from her own language.

A further problem experienced by informants was the perceived relationship between student and instructor, providing support for Smoke (1988), who found that 81 percent of her informants expressed difficulty in "talking to the professors" (p. 13). Fernanda, for example, felt that instructors put themselves above their students, which had the effect of making it difficult for her to feel comfortable approaching an instructor for needed help. Ayla had difficulty in speaking directly to her instructor, something that she perceived as being necessary in the American context, because she had been taught all her life to speak indirectly to her instructors and not ask them questions directly. Additionally, Fernanda reported having difficulty in getting used to her instructor's voices, especially the quality of their voices. For Mari, the problem manifested itself in the fact that she felt that it would be inappropriate to ask questions of her instructor since it would "interrupt" the flow of the class. Additionally, Lyn reported that she had a difficult time matching her schedule with her teacher's schedule and therefore had a hard time meeting with that instructor, which made it difficult to get the help that she needed.

Sixty-eight percent of the informants in Ostler's study reported the need to ask questions. However, asking questions also posed a problem for the informants. For Samory, a lack of knowledge of Soil Resources hampered his ability to ask questions. While he felt that asking questions in class was one of the best ways for him to learn, he felt that the lack of background knowledge prevented him from asking such questions. Kelley & Sweet (1991) write, regarding the students in their study, "It has become clear that these students often know the correct answer, or have their homework assignment completed, but lack the confidence to speak aloud in class. They worry about being the 'only person with an accent' or that the teacher and other students will not understand them" (p. 6). For Mari, asking questions in front of large groups proved to be impossible because of fear of being embarrassed. Lyn was also greatly affected in that she felt that she didn't know how to form the questions that she needed to ask, thereby missing valuable chances for extra help.

Testing styles also caused difficulties for the informants. Ostler found that 45 percent of the informants in her survey reported the need to take multiple choice tests. For Samory, who was accustomed to taking essay tests, multiple choice questions caused problems since he had never had to complete such types of questions before. Ostler also found that 48 percent of the informants needed the ability to take essay exams. In contrast to Samory, Fernanda had experience with multiple choice tests, but had never had the previous experience of taking essay tests. Lack of experience with certain testing styles thus made studying for certain types of tests difficult, as well as making it difficult to complete certain parts of tests, thereby lowering informants' grades and not accurately reflecting their true state of knowledge. Romulo also reported that the way in which questions were asked in his Public Relations course also caused him problems, in that he had a difficult time in understanding the subtle differences in the way that his instructor used vocabulary on tests and quizzes. While he had an easy time remembering the larger concepts, he had a difficult time remembering the exact subtle differences in the meanings of the vocabulary.

Different styles of reading materials also affected informants, especially undergraduates. In her study, Harklau (1994) found that input in the form of reading was plentiful, but was somewhat lacking in variety. Textbooks were the predominant source of reading material for most students. Both Mari and Romulo, however, were required to read historical narratives, historical novels, and books of poetry. While they had experience and training in reading textbooks through the IEP, they had a difficult time reading these alternative types of texts, since they had no experience with them. These texts also caused problems in that they assumed previous knowledge that the informants didn't possess.

A lack of understanding of cultural significance also caused difficulties for some of the informants. Ostler (1980) writes, "As noted by Selinker, Todd-Trimble & Trimble (1976) students can often understand the words and the sentences, yet not comprehend the total meaning of technical discourse" (p. 492). Mari, for example, had problems in writing business letters. While she understood the individual words and grammar of individual sentences, she could not understand the meanings that lay behind the word choices or letter styles, lacking the cultural understanding of why she should use certain words and styles in certain situations. For Samory, the difficulty arose when his instructor used examples that came only from the United States, a cultural situation that he did not understand well, and therefore had a hard time applying to the situation in his own country, a situation that he would return to in the near future.

A further problem experienced by Fernanda was that she came into her program in the middle of the school year. Because she had entered her program at mid-year, she did not have the orientation to the program that those entering at the beginning of the school year had been given. Additionally, as a graduate student whose classes were sequenced, she lacked certain knowledge that her classmates had acquired during the previous semester, which put her at a disadvantage in what she perceived as the very competitive environment of her major, an atmosphere that she was unaccustomed to.

A large problem for Mari was that she felt that there was a large gap between what she had learned in her advanced writing class in the IEP and the basic writing class that she took from the English department. This is very similar to the findings of Atkinson & Ramanathan (1995), in their comparison of writing instruction in an English language program and the writing instruction of a university composition program. Atkinson & Ramanathan found that the university composition program presupposed cultural knowledge that couldn't be reasonably attributed to the non-native speakers and that while the English language program attempted to promote "workmanlike prose," the university composition program emphasized "sophisticated thought and expression" (pp. 559-560). Students would thus, they write, "experience a significant disjuncture between the way each program conceptualizes writing" (563). It was obvious that Mari was experiencing just such a "disjuncture" and that she therefore felt that there should be a much greater connection between the two programs when it comes to writing.

Several additional problems occurred, as noted earlier. Large class sizes were also a problem for both Mari and Romulo. Mari and Romulo also were required to take courses that they felt would not be of use to them in the future. Samory, likewise, was taking courses that he lacked interest in, and therefore lacked motivation in studying. Lack of background knowledge in certain courses was also a problem for several informants. For Samory, examples taken only from the context of the United States, a context that he did not understand well, also caused problems, as did the lack of examples in mathematics class for Lyn.

6. What actions on the part of informants helped to make the transition smoother?

While having a network of friends outside of class, especially friends from their home countries, was helpful in the early stages of the semester, one of the most important actions on the part of informants that proved beneficial was to develop a network of friends within their classes from whom the informants were able to get information and advice, as well as with whom they could discuss homework, research projects, and presentations. This was especially important for informants when they were just beginning a project or doing research. Also helpful in this area was to develop connections with people who were more advanced in their program and who were able to give advice on what to expect in the future and how they should prepare for upcoming classes. For several of the informants, getting together with classmates to study and compare notes proved beneficial in that they were better able to study for tests, as in the case of Romulo and Fernanda, or were better able to ask questions in class, as in the case of Samory, since he was able to practice asking questions with his classmates beforehand. For Ayla, this network of classmates made it easier and more effective for her when giving instructions in the Cello Sectional.

Another action on the part of informants that was helpful in making the transition smoother was to take advantage of all extra help that was given. For

Mari and Romulo, for example, both of whom were undergraduates, this meant attending review sessions for their courses. By taking advantage of these opportunities, informants were able to ask questions in more comfortable settings, as well as to gather valuable information on how tests would be structured and what materials to study for the tests. It was also helpful in giving more immediate feedback on assignments, such as on written assignments during Romulo's visits to the Learning Center. This extra help also involved getting a set of lecture notes from the instructor, as in the case of Mari.

A further action on the part of informants that was beneficial was to position themselves within the classroom in a way that was productive. Harklau (1994) writes, "Many teachers had learned through experience to place ESL students in desks close to the front of the room so that they could scan students' faces for signs of comprehension, confusion, or responses to questions" (p. 250). It is apparent through this study that former IEP students need to foster this connection with their instructors on their own. In large classes especially, by positioning themselves at the front of the classroom, for example, informants were able to take better notes, to make recordings of lectures, to ask questions, and to tune out the noise and distractions made by the rest of the students in the class. It also allowed the informants to develop better relationships with their instructors, as in the case of Romulo. For Fernanda, this also involved placing herself at the front of the class so that she could record lectures for later playback and transcription to fill in notes taken during class. Also beneficial, as mentioned previously, was keeping a positive attitude toward study and seeing difficulties as opportunities.

Smoke (1988) found that 92 percent of those she surveyed said that they had difficulty "understanding how to read and study from textbooks" (p. 13). This was also a problem for the informants in the present study. A further action that helped informants, however, was the realization that they needed to read selectively and not try to read everything that was assigned to them. This developed out of the large amount of reading that was assigned to them and the pressure from the lack of time that all of the informants were experiencing. By attempting, at the beginning of the semester, to read everything that was assigned to them, informants fell behind in their readings and assignments and spent the remainder of the semester attempting to catch up with reading. By being more critical over which materials they needed to read, informants were able to be, as Ayla put it, "more efficient." This also involved reading the material more than once, as in the case of Lyn, who felt that she needed to read the material before the lecture, to understand what the instructor was talking about, then again after the lecture so that she could remember the material.

Several actions were taken on the part of informants that greatly assisted in making the transition smoother. One helpful strategy was to approach the instructor of a course immediately at the beginning of the course, as Romulo did, explaining that he was not a native speaker of English and that therefore his assignments might contain language errors. By approaching the instructor beforehand, Romulo was able to explain that the errors were not because of lack of intelligence, lack of effort, or lack of interest in the course, but rather because English was not his native language. Other actions included asking the instructor for extra work that would offset low grades on tests, as in the case of Samory, or asking instructors for sets of course notes, as in the case of Mari.

Another helpful action on the part of several informants was to seek extra help in pronunciation by attending the Speech Pathology Department's speech lab. This supports the work of Smoke (1988), who found that when asked what course they would add to the ESL sequence, 27 percent, the largest response, responded with the need to add a pronunciation course, with 23 percent saying they wanted a speech course. From this, Smoke believed that "students who responded to the questionnaire by stating that they want pronunciation and speech courses seem to be asking for more participation in college. They want to be able to ask or answer questions in front of native speaking counterparts and feel comfortable in the classroom." (p. 15). Attendance at the speech lab not only helped informants with their pronunciation, but it also in turn gave informants more confidence in speaking in front of large groups, such as during a presentation, and confidence in asking questions during class.

Informants also indicated that they planned to take several actions in the future that they felt would make their course work smoother. One of these steps involved putting more energy into the beginning of the semester to ensure that they did not fall behind in the early stages, which would forced them to play catch-up all semester long. This was especially true in the case of reading. Informants also planned to read ahead in their courses, using the time between semesters to read the textbooks that they were to use for the following semester. In this way, they felt, they would be better prepared for what the instructor was going to talk about and would also be better able to retain the information when reading it a second time. Informants also expressed plans to be more forceful in expressing their opinions in the future, especially in such things as group projects. Samory also commented that he would choose more familiar topics in the future.

7. What actions on the part of informants caused the most difficulties in making the transition?

An action on the part of informants that caused difficulty in making the transition was the fact that they waited too long to begin working in earnest at the beginning of the semester, especially waiting too long to begin doing the reading that was assigned to them. Because they found that each part of the course was built off previously covered material, if they did not understand the initial material, they had a difficult time following subsequent materials. This forced them to play "catch up" the entire semester. However, with the already small amount of time available, this put added strain on them in that it left less time to complete projects and study for tests. This in turn left them with less time to read, continuing the cycle. Fernanda also expressed a need to start earlier on projects.

Conversely, Ayla tried to do too much at the beginning of the semester and ended up putting too much physical stress on herself, resulting in an injury to her wrist.

Further, several informants reported initially attempting to read all of the material that was assigned to them. In the words of Ayla, they were "inefficient" readers. As the semester progressed, the informants found that it was impossible to read everything that they had been assigned, instead needing to be much more selective about what they read.

A further problem on the part of Mari was simply taking too many classes and misunderstanding what was entailed in the classes she was going to take. Because of the large number of classes that she was taking, she felt that she was not able to put enough focus and energy into the classes that would really help her in her major. She also made the mistake of selecting the wrong classes. In that case of her Volleyball class, for example, she thought that she would just be playing volleyball. However, the course was actually for those who planned to teach physical education and thus entailed research and writing long papers, which demanded a great deal of effort on her part and further took time and energy away from her other courses.

Failure to develop a network of classmates on the part of Mari also caused problems for her. She reported that she never discussed any of her class work with her classmates. She also reported that none of her friends had taken any of the courses that she was taking at the time of the study and that they therefore could not be helpful to her. Instead, she resorted to studying on her own, which was not beneficial.

On the contrary, however, dependence on classmates also caused problems, as in the case of Lyn. She reported that she often asked for help, not only from classmates, but from others from her home country who were more advanced in her program. Because of this over-dependency on classmates and asking for help from them too often, she felt that she didn't learn how to do things on her own or to think for herself, which she felt would hurt her when she entered the workplace and had to complete work on her own.

Smoke found that 74 percent of those responding to her survey had trouble taking notes from lecture classes. This was apparent in the present study as well, in the sense that an action on the part of informants that was detrimental was to attempt to take word-for-word notes of an instructor's lecture, focusing on the words, rather than larger concepts. Tied in with this was the excessive use of a dictionary to look up words, as in the case of Mari. By the time Mari had looked up a word, the instructor would be on to a new part of the lecture and the larger meaning of the lecture would be lost on her.

Ostler found that 41 percent of the informants in her study reported the need to give talks in class. Informants, however, also had difficulties in expressing their opinions in front of others, especially in front of large groups. Given the large amount of group work involved, however, this caused them great difficulties. In the case of Mari, she had difficulty in providing verbal responses quickly, since that would be considered rude behavior in her home country. Ayla had a hard time being forceful with her opinions, having been taught to be indirect in expressing her opinions. Additionally, Fernanda felt that her opinions were ignored because she was an international student; this in turn made her angry, which then caused her to withdraw from participation in her group.

A further action on the part of informants that was detrimental was being too timid in asking questions in class, as in the case of Mari, and being too timid in expressing their opinions, as reported by Ayla and Fernanda, for fear of embarrassment. As Rubin (1975) has written, "The good language learner is often not inhibited. He is willing to appear foolish if communication results. He is willing to make mistakes in order to learn and to communicate" (p. 41).

8. What actions on the part of instructors helped to make the transition smoother?

One action on the part of instructors that helped the informants greatly was to provide a model of a process for the informants. This was especially helpful for informants who had difficulty asking questions in front of large groups, such as Mari and Lyn, since they were much more comfortable in one-to-one interactions with an instructor. It was also beneficial for informants who had difficulty constructing questions, such as Lyn, since she was able to refer directly to the process or to examples of the process. It was also helpful to those informants who considered themselves hands-on learners, such as Romulo. Repetition of terms in dance class also helped Ayla learn the terms more easily. For Fernanda, the modeling that was beneficial was the modeling on the part of instructors of how to be a professional in her field.

A further action on the part of instructors that was beneficial was to provide extra materials for the informants, such as an outline on an overhead at the beginning of class, as in the case of Romulo, or a packet of course notes, as in the case of Samory, which provided a conceptual framework for the informant to follow during lectures and allowed them to focus on the ideas of the lecture, rather than attempting word-for-word note taking. A beneficial action on the part of an instructor for Mari was giving her a set of class notes so that she could more easily follow the lecture without being forced to look up words in the dictionary.

Also proving beneficial on the part of instructors was to make sure that everyone in the course understood the material before moving on to new material, as in the case of Lyn, whose teacher would explain things "step by step," supporting Shuck (1995), who writes that we should "give students more time to practice what they have learned before moving on" (p. 44). This was especially important for those informants who had difficulty expressing opinions or asking questions in front of large groups or had difficulty in formulating questions. It was also helpful in that it more closely matched the teaching style of teachers from the informants' home countries. Harklau (1994) has found that this was one of the major differences between mainstream and ESL courses.

Allowing the informants extra time on tests and allowing them to do extra work to compensate for poor performances on tests was also beneficial. This was especially important for informants who were not used to expressing their opinions quickly, as in the case of Mari, or used to timed tests, as in the case of Samory, but rather were used to situations where they were able to give considerable thought to a problem or question before answering. Also beneficial to Lyn were the additional materials that her computer instructor would place on the computers for students to work through, since it provided additional models, which was a method that she felt helped her learn best.

9. What actions on the part of instructors caused the most difficulties in making the transition?

The biggest obstacle on the part of instructors came from the differences in underlying philosophies of teaching that they brought to the classroom. Rather than expecting the students to memorize names and dates in history, as in the case of Mari, for example, her instructor expected her to understand and interpret the deeper underlying issues. In Lyn's math classes, students were expected to not only memorize formulas and examples, but to understand the concepts behind the formulas as well. These different philosophies also manifested themselves in how the informants perceived the student-teacher relationship. In the case of Fernanda, for example, she felt that instructors in America placed themselves above their students, which was different from the equal status that she perceived to exist in her home country.

The examples, or lack of examples, that instructors brought to the classroom could also prove problematic. For Lyn, a lack of examples in mathematics or computer science caused problems, since she was accustomed in her home country to instructors giving large numbers of examples for students to learn from. For Samory, examples in his Environmental Economics class were all from the United States, not from his home country. He felt that since he did not fully understand the American context, it was difficult for him to understand the example and that therefore he would have a difficult time applying the example to his home country in the future.

Two further problems were also identified by Harklau (1994), who writes, "Learners were also frustrated with teachers who habitually spoke very fast, who used frequent asides, or who were prone to sudden departures from the instructional topic at hand" (p. 249). A problem on the part of an instructor in the case of Lyn, in this area, was that one of her instructors spoke at a very rapid rate. This follows Harklau (1994) who found that "because they were primarily addressing native speakers of English, mainstream high school classroom teachers seldom adjusted input in order to make it comprehensible to L2 learners" (p. 249). For Fernanda, it was also very frustrating when her Public Issues instructor would deviate from the stated topic. When the instructor followed the outline given before class, Fernanda had no difficulty following his lectures. When he deviated from this outline, however, she had difficulties understanding him.

For Fernanda, a problem on the part of her Public Issues instructor was that he inadvertently placed all inexperienced students, except for one student, in the same group, a group which was required to complete a group project and then give a formal presentation based on that project. This was especially problematic for her since she had never seen a formal presentation before and had no concept of what one should look like. Without a strong leader to provide that concept, she felt lost while completing the project and didn't know how to contribute to the group.

A further problem identified by Samory occurred on the part of his instructor in reaction to Samory's difficulty in taking certain types of exams. The instructor, rather than recognizing Samory's difficulties as a product of test anxiety, made the assumption that the difficulties were due to a language deficiency on the part of Samory, going so far as to recommend remedial English language training. Samory was adamant, however, in his claim that his difficulties arose from unfamiliarity with the test types, and not from lack of knowledge about the topic, or lack of language skills. The assumption that it was a language problem only further added to Samory's test anxiety. Based on Samory's experience, it is easy to agree with Horowitz, etal. (1986), who write, "Teachers should always consider the possibility that anxiety is responsible for the student behaviors . . . before attributing poor student performance solely to lack of ability, inadequate background, or poor motivation" (p. 131).

10. What areas could the Intensive English Program improve on to make the transition smoother?

One of the areas most cited by the informants that needed improvement on the part of the IEP was to do more work with presentations. Ostler found that 41 percent of the informants in her study reported the need to give talks in class. Informants in the present study felt that the form that this work should take should be varied. They felt they needed practice presenting formally in front of large groups, such as presenting the results of a group project, but also informally in front of smaller groups, as in a peer group situation. Held in common was the idea that informants needed practice in front of Americans, not just in front of IEP instructors or other students in the IEP. As Perdreau (1994) points out, intensive English programs "provide a nurturing, culturally sensitive environment that can go a great distance toward helping international students adapt to the new, English-dominant surroundings" (cited in Shuck, 1995). The people in the IEP, however, in informants' opinions, could be "too nice" and would too easily understand the mistakes that the informants made. All informants in the study wanted to have the practice of presenting in front of Americans, but felt that it would be best to begin slowly, first in front of other students from the IEP, then perhaps other instructors from the IEP, then moving slowly, step-by-step, to presenting in front of Americans.

Further, a majority of the informants in the study felt that they needed practice in doing group work. Ostler found that 35 percent of those responding to her survey reported the need to participate in panel discussions. By practicing in groups, informants believed, they could learn to more easily express their opinions in a way that would make their American counterparts comfortable and in such a way that Americans would accept those ideas. It would also allow them to have practice dealing with people that they might not necessarily like. Additionally, it would allow them to see the cultural differences between group work in their countries and group work in America. Once again, informants felt that they needed practice in front of "real Americans," not just others from the IEP, who would be too understanding, but also felt that this transition should take place slowly.

In the same way, informants felt that it was important for IEP students to have practice listening and speaking to Americans, not just IEP classmates who were too understanding. Informants also felt that it was important to listen to someone other than their IEP instructors, since they quickly became conditioned to their instructors' voices, but experienced difficulty when attempting to transfer this listening ability to new mainstream instructors. Several informants also expressed the belief that IEP instructors were easier to understand than their mainstream instructors. Further, informants also felt that listening to tapes of lectures was not sufficient, since real-life lectures were filled with much more imperfect speech than the tapes were. Once again, informants suggested beginning with an instructor, then moving slowly toward the speech of other Americans. This situation could also provide practice taking notes from a lecture, they felt.

Also of importance was formal instruction in how to formulate questions, especially in front of large groups, but also in one-to-one interaction with an instructor. By practicing how to more easily formulate questions, informants felt that they could more easily express their opinions in the faster American way. As expressed by Lyn, this practice should consist both of learning the mechanics of question formation, as well as the cultural underpinnings of what different questions involved, as well as when and where to ask questions so that they would not be seen as impolite.

A further suggestion for the IEP was to have writing instructors provide more immediate feedback on written assignments, rather than delayed feedback as was the norm. In this way, informants would be able to make better revisions and to more easily remember the things that they had learned. Informants also felt that the writing assignments should be more closely related to their individual majors, which would be more "efficient" and would make students happier, since it would help them see how things worked in their majors.

Just as it was felt that writing could be more closely tied to informants' majors, a majority of informants also thought that reading could be more closely tied to their majors. This, they felt, would make the learning of vocabulary easier and more meaningful. This was especially important, they felt, given the large amount of reading that they had to do. It would also, once again, be more "efficient" and would serve to make IEP students happier and thus more motivated to learn.

Further suggestions included practice with different types of tests, since in their mainstream classes they were encountering tests that were of different types than they were accustomed to in their home countries. These tests could be implemented, they felt, in any of the various IEP courses. Students should also be exposed to different types of texts, especially undergraduate students, and not just textbooks, since they would be expected to read and respond to these different kinds of texts in mainstream courses.

Suggestions also included giving students a more formal introduction to the academic environment of an American university and, in general, providing more interaction with Americans. In this way, informants felt that they would not experience as much culture shock while making the transition. Also, instituting a more formal system of helping students once they had left the IEP was thought to be beneficial. This, they felt, would give them confidence, since they would know that there was someone to turn to that they could talk with in case of an emergency or difficulty.

Overall, informants expressed a need to connect the various IEP classes to a greater degree to the individual students' majors. Informants all felt that this connection should occur in all IEP classes. For Fernanda, this connection was necessary so that students could become more familiar with vocabulary from their majors. For Lyn, this connection would serve to make IEP classes "more efficient," which would in turn serve to make IEP students happier and more motivated to study.

CHAPTER SIX
SUMMARY OF THE RESEARCH, SUGGESTIONS FOR INTENSIVE ENGLISH PROGRAMS, AND RECOMMENDATIONS FOR FURTHER RESEARCH

Introduction

This Chapter will first provide a summary of the research, reviewing the purpose of the study, the informants studied, and the methodology used, then providing a summarized version of the major findings of the study. Suggestions for actions to be taken by intensive English programs will then be given, followed by recommendations for further research.

The Purpose of the Study

This ethnographic study examines the processes that six informants went through as they made the transition from an intensive English program to mainstream university courses. It attempts to determine what needs such students have as they make this transition, as well as what actions on the part of students, instructors, and intensive English programs can help make such a transition more effective and smooth. This study proposes to provide a more accurate description of the articulation process than has previously been given, providing data on what students go through from their perspective, in their terms. Additionally, it advocates ways in which intensive English programs can prepare students for, and assist students in, making the transition.

The Informants

Six informants were chosen for the purposes of this study. Three of the informants were undergraduate students, three graduate students. Informants ranged in age from 20 to 34. Informants were all chosen from the pool of students enrolled in an intensive English program in the Department of English at a medium-sized Midwestern university during the fall semester of 1998. The informants were selected on the basis of their advanced status in the intensive English program. They were all students who were in their final semester of the program, were ready to enroll in mainstream university courses, but had not yet enrolled in such courses. These informants were chosen from a list of all possible students in the program who fit the criteria.

Methodology

The primary means of data gathering for this study was through ethnographic informant interviews, all of which were held in the researcher's office in the intensive English program. This provided an easily accessible place to meet the informants, as well as a place where interviews could easily and quietly be tape recorded. All interviews occurred at the convenience of the informants.

Informants were first given a complete description of the nature of the interview questions to be asked. A rationale for why certain types of questions were to be asked was also given. The types of questions asked in these interviews ranged from relatively closed-ended questions from prepared interview schedules to more open-ended questions based on responses gathered during previous interviews.

The first purpose of the initial interview sequence, which was conducted in two parts, was to clarify the nature of the study, as well as to explain the risks and benefits for the informants involved. Informants were informed that the interviews would be tape recorded and that after each interview, a transcription of each tape would be made. Risks were explained to them, which included the loss of time spent in the interview, time that could otherwise have been spent studying. Benefits were also explained, which included helping them gain insight into the experiences that they were having as they made the transition from the intensive English program to mainstream university courses, as well as helping the program and intensive English programs in general. Informants were also informed that their real names would not appear in any publication or presentation based on the study.

Subsequent interviews were conducted at three to four week intervals during the semester in which informants first began their mainstream university courses. In these interviews, informants were first asked to describe their mainstream courses, detailing what they were encountering in each class, as well as describing what obstacles they were meeting. As the semester progressed, more individualized issues were addressed and more individualized questions were asked of the informants, based on issues and concerns that they had raised in previous interviews. Informants were also given the chance to express their opinions on what they believed they could have done better in making the transition, as well as what they believed intensive English program could have done to better prepare them for mainstream courses. Classroom observations for each of the informants were also carried out during the semester. These observations were made to obtain a first hand verification of statements made by the informants.

After each interview, transcriptions of each tape recording were made. These transcriptions were then coded, based on a modified version of the Outline of Cultural Materials. A journal was also kept that recorded independent observations, research design changes, a schedule of interviews, areas to be covered in subsequent interviews, and specific questions to be asked.

Findings

1. What variables in the background of the informants were the most helpful in making the transition?

For many of the informants in the study, previous knowledge, especially of vocabulary, was the most beneficial variable in their background experience. Regardless of whether the knowledge was gained formally or informally, it gave the informants confidence and made them feel that they could focus on the content and issues of the course, rather than being forced to focus so heavily on the language of the course. It also allowed them to ask questions, which in turn furthered their learning.

Having a developed network of friends and family also proved to be beneficial, especially at the beginning of the semester. This type of support took many forms, including others from the informants' home countries, especially those who were in the same program, and support from family members. Previous exposure to American culture also proved beneficial, whether in America or through exposure to Americans back in the home culture of the informants. Also of benefit was keeping a positive attitude about the learning situation.

2. What variables in the background of the informants caused the most difficulties in making the transition?

Contrasting the positive effect of previous knowledge, a lack of background experiences in certain subjects had detrimental effects. Because of lack of exposure to a subject, informants felt that they were at a disadvantage compared to their classmates, who came to the class with more background knowledge. It also caused problems in that informants were not able to ask questions, which kept them from learning in a way that they thought productive. Lack of background knowledge was especially detrimental when it came to vocabulary.

Lack of knowledge of how to conduct library research also proved problematic. Informants perceived the size of The University's library to be much larger than libraries in their home countries and that there were too many materials to examine while conducting research. Also problematic was the use of the library's computer system, which informants felt was time consuming and difficult.

The process of conducting research in general was also held to be problematic. The abstract nature and broad range of research topics was tied in with a lack of background knowledge, the wide range of materials to cover, and anxiety about technology, making research a difficult process for informants. Particularly difficult were the early stages of research, where informants felt that they "didn't know where to begin."

Anxiety about technology also surfaced in general computer use. Informants felt that they either lacked any experience using computers or that if they had experience, they lacked a formal terminology with which to discuss and ask questions about computer use.

Lack of exposure to certain types of tests also caused difficulties for some informants. This lack of exposure caused several problems. Informants were sometimes unable to judge how much time a test would take, and therefore ran out of time while taking the test. It also caused problems in that it made it difficult to decide how to study for a test, leaving informants unable to answer certain questions on tests.

Lack of exposure to certain types of text styles was also problematic for some informants, especially undergraduates. While they were accustomed to the style of textbooks, other text styles were problematic, especially those that assumed previous knowledge that the informants did not possess, such as historical novels and historical narratives.

Also causing problems for informants was their lack of exposure to certain types of teaching styles and course expectations. Different underlying philosophies about the learning of history or mathematics, for example, caused problems. In history, informants were expected not only to memorize names and dates, but to interpret history as well. In mathematics, they were expected to not only memorize formulas, but to understand the theory behind the formulas as well.

Understanding how to interact with instructors was also problematic. Differences in perceptions of the teacher-student relationship caused problems, as did differences in speaking directly with an instructor.

A further problem for several of the informants was difficulty in asking questions. This was a problem in that several informants felt intimidated by large class sizes and by speaking in front of groups, as well as having difficulty in knowing how to construct questions. Also proving problematic was difficulty in understanding underlying cultural meanings.

3. Do undergraduate and graduate students go through similar or different processes as they make the transition?

The size of classes encountered seemed to be one of the largest differences between the experiences of undergraduate students versus graduate students. While graduate students had relatively small classes, undergraduates had to contend with much larger class sizes. Large class sizes meant more distractions and noise to deal with, making it more difficult to understand the instructor's lecture and take notes. It also made it very difficult for some informants to ask questions in class, since they were intimidated by large groups.

Another major difference was that while graduate students primarily took courses that were in their major, undergraduate students were also required to take a certain number of courses to meet general credit requirements. This caused informants to feel that they were learning things that they would not be able to use in the future and that they were forced to take time and energy away from the courses in their major, learning large amounts of vocabulary that they would not use in the future. It also created the problem that students were taking classes that did not meet their initial expectations. Undergraduate students, on the other hand, had a wider number of support structures to choose from, including review sessions and tutoring through the Learning Center.

On the other hand, graduate students were sometimes too limited in the number of courses they could take. Since they had much more directed goals in mind, any class that was not directly related to that goal was deemed unnecessary. And because the courses were much more prescriptively sequenced, coming in to the program at the middle of the school year also caused problems. Graduate students were also expected to take a much greater leadership role.

4. What variables encountered in the environment were the most helpful in making the transition?

A variable encountered in the environment that was helpful to the informants was being able to do hands-on work, such as while sitting at a computer terminal. This was beneficial since it more closely matched the learning styles of certain informants, as well as making it easier for informants to formulate and ask questions directly of their instructors.

Time in their individual classes and programs also proved beneficial to the informants in that they were able to become accustomed to their instructors' teaching styles, presentation styles, test types, text types, and instructors' voices. As they progressed through their classes, they began to better understand their instructors' expectations.

Having previous experience working with Americans also proved beneficial in that informants were more familiar with the American style of writing. Also helpful was the willingness on the part of departments to give extra help to informants when needed.

5. What variables encountered in the environment caused the most difficulties in making the transition?

Lack of time to complete all reading and homework assignments was the primary variable that caused problems for the informants. While informants felt that the readings they were assigned were not difficult, the large amount of reading assigned to them meant that they had a hard time completing assignments, which in turn left little time to study for tests. Especially problematic was the fact that informants started reading late and then spent the rest of the semester attempting to catch up, which put them further behind, leaving little time to complete projects or study for tests.

Also problematic was the large amount of group work that they were required to complete. While group work came in many forms, certain problems were found to be common. Informants had a difficult time sharing their work with others, had a difficult time expressing their opinions in front of large groups of people, and felt that they lacked the cultural understanding of how groups worked in America.

Closely related to the problems with group work were problems in giving presentations. These presentations also took many different forms, yet had consistent problems. Informants had a difficult time expressing opinions in presentation form, had difficulty in conceiving how a formal presentation should work, and felt unsure about their topics, fearing the questions that their audiences would ask.

Doing research also caused problems, especially given the perceived large size of the library and the complexity of using the library's computer system. Also problematic were the broad nature of research topics and difficulty in knowing how to narrow topics down, as well as difficulty in knowing how to get started on research projects.

Note taking also was a problem when informants were too dependent on dictionaries or attempted to take word-for-word notes. Differences in testing styles and text styles also caused problems for informants, who were not used to different styles in their backgrounds. Lack of cultural understanding also posed a problem.

A further problem was difficulty in understanding the relationship between student and instructor. This caused difficulty in knowing how to approach and discuss course work with instructors and feeling uncomfortable in asking them for needed help. This was especially true for those informants who came from cultures where students would normally be expected to speak more indirectly to instructors.

Asking questions in class also posed a problem, especially for those informants who felt that asking questions was the best way for them to learn. Difficulties with different testing styles and different text styles also caused difficulty for those who were unfamiliar with the types.

Also causing difficulty for one graduate student informant was that she came into her program in the middle of the school year. Because the classes that she was taking were sequenced, she felt that she lacked knowledge that her classmates had acquired the previous semester, which put her at a disadvantage.

Also causing a problem for one undergraduate informant was the perceived large gap between what she had learned in her IEP writing class and what she was learning in her basic writing class in the mainstream English department.

6. What actions on the part of informants helped to make the transition smoother?

One of the most important actions on the part of informants was to develop a network of friends within their classes, in addition to the network of friends and family that they had outside of their classes. This was important because it gave the informants the chance to discuss their homework assignments, research projects, presentations, and tests. It also helped them overcome misperceptions about Americans.

Taking advantage of all extra help offered was also beneficial to the informants. By taking advantage of such things as review sessions or free tutoring, informants were better able to ask questions in comfortable settings, get information on how tests would be structured, and find out what materials to study for individual tests. It also provided informants with immediate feedback on assignments.

Situating themselves in beneficial positions also proved helpful to informants. In this way, informants were better able to tune out the noise and distractions of large classes, take better notes, ask questions more easily, and to develop better relationships with their instructors.

The recognition that they had to read selectively also proved beneficial for informants. By reading more selectively, informants were able to have more time to complete homework, group work, and presentation assignments, which in turn freed up more time for studying for tests.

Other beneficial actions were also taken by informants. Approaching the instructor at the beginning of the semester to explain their linguistic situation was particularly effective, resulting in a better relationship with the instructor as well as garnering additional help from the instructor. Seeking extra help in pronunciation from the Speech Pathology Department's speech lab also proved highly beneficial in that it gave informants greater confidence in asking questions and speaking in front of large groups.

Putting more time and energy into reading at the beginning of the semester was a further action that informants planned to take in the future. By doing this, they would avoid falling behind initially, and would then avoid the need to play catch up all semester, leaving them more time for homework assignments and studying for tests. This included reading ahead for future courses between semesters.

7. What actions on the part of informants caused the most difficulties in making the transition?

Waiting too long to get started working in earnest at the beginning of the semester caused the greatest difficulties, especially waiting too long to get started reading. Because of the large amount of reading that informants had to do, by falling behind during the initial stages of the semester, informants had a hard time completing homework assignments, which left little time to study for tests. Further, attempting to read all readings assigned to them was also problematic.

Failure to develop a network of friends in classes also proved detrimental. Without this network of friends, there was no one to discuss homework assignments, projects, and tests with. Conversely, however, too much dependence on classmates also proved problematic in that one informant did not learn how to complete projects on her own, which she realized would cause problems for her later when she entered the workplace.

Attempting to take word-for-word notes also was problematic, as was excessively looking up words in the dictionary. This took time away from the lecture; by the time the word was looked up, the instructor would have moved ahead in the lecture and the student would become lost. By taking word-for-word notes, informants were loosing the overall meaning of the lecture. Being too timid in asking questions or expressing opinions for fear of embarrassment also caused problems.

8. What actions on the part of instructors helped to make the transition smoother?

Instructors providing a model for students to follow proved helpful to the informants. This was especially helpful for those informants who had a hard time asking questions in front of a large group, in that they could ask the questions in a one-to-one setting, and for those informants who had a hands-on learning style.

Also beneficial was to provide extra materials for the informants, such as an outline on an overhead or a packet of notes to follow, both of which provided a conceptual framework for the informants to follow, allowing them to focus on the main ideas of the lecture rather than word-for-word notes.

Making sure that everyone understood the material before moving on was another action by instructors that proved beneficial, especially for those informants who had a difficult time asking questions in front of groups and for those informants who came from countries with a similar teaching style. Allowing extra time on tests or allowing informants to perform extra tasks to raise their grades also proved helpful.

9. What actions on the part of instructors caused the most difficulties in making the transition?

Instructors with different underlying philosophies about the learning process caused the most difficulty for informants. While informants came from systems where they were primarily expected to memorize facts and figures, their instructors in America expected them to interpret and understand the concepts and theories discussed in their classes, which led to difficulties for many of the informants.

Examples that were used in classes could also be problematic, either from the perspective of a lack of examples or because the examples were all pulled from the context of the United States, a context that informants did not understand as well as contexts from their own countries or that they felt they could not apply in their home countries in the future. Instructors who spoke very fast and who had frequently straying from the topic at hand also made it difficult for informants to understand lectures.

In addition, on the part of one informant, a problem was caused when an instructor mistakenly attributed difficulty on exams to a lack of knowledge of language, rather than to language anxiety, as it was viewed by the informant.

10. What areas could the Intensive English Program improve on to make the transition smoother?

Informants felt strongly that the IEP needs to do more work with both presentations and group work. The form that this practice should take should be varied, since informants were coming in contact with many different forms of both. Informants felt in all cases, however, that fellow IEP students and IEP instructors were much too kind and understood their problems too easily, and that therefore practice should be given in front of Americans, since they would be meeting and interacting with them in mainstream environments. This process needed to be done in stages, however, informants felt. In the same way, informants also wanted practice speaking with and listening to Americans, especially practice in listening to real life lectures, which could then give them practice in taking lecture notes. Informants also felt that it was important to have practice in formulating questions, especially in front of large groups, thereby helping them to better express their opinions.

More immediate feedback on written work was also deemed important, since it was felt that this feedback helped them learn better. Also, tying in writing assignments and reading assignments more closely to their majors was felt to be important, which would help them pre-learn the vocabulary of their majors, as well as give them an idea of how things worked in their majors.

Practice with different types of testing styles and text styles was also suggested, as was a more formal introduction to American academic culture. A more formal system of helping students once they had left the IEP was also suggested.

Suggestions for intensive English programs

While intensive English programs can play, as mentioned in the previous chapter, "a facilitative role in the formation of peer networks and adjustments to

U.S. school and society" (Harklau, 1994, p. 265), the programmatic needs of the IEP may lead to a misconception on the part of students regarding the pace of assignments at the very beginning of the semester. Because of the testing that is necessary to be conducted and the need to place students at the correct level, students in the IEP are discouraged from purchasing their books until approximately the middle of the second week of the semester. This situation may perhaps give students the impression that the real work in an American university does not truly begin until the semester is well underway. In mainstream classes, however, the informants in this study were expected to read large amounts of material, literally from the beginning of the semester. Because the informants were unaware of this fact, they delayed getting started reading in earnest, which put them almost immediately behind in reading. This in turn put a great deal of strain on their already limited time, forcing them to play catch up for the remainder of the semester. For this reason, therefore, it is apparent that the IEP needs to make it clear to students how much work will be expected of them from the beginning of the semester.

Because students will need to immediately interact with materials in mainstream courses, it is apparent that intensive English programs need to provide students with more time to explore their individual majors before they enter mainstream university programs and that IEP classes need to be linked to mainstream classes to a greater degree. While numerous programs exist, such as those following the sheltered model, theme-based model, or adjunct model described in Chapter I, the present research suggests that such models would not meet the needs of the informants in the study, since their experiences were so diverse, with each informant's transition shaped to a great degree by their academic major. This seemed to be especially true in the area of vocabulary development. Therefore, it is apparent that what is needed is to develop IEP courses, especially in the areas of reading and writing, that would require the students to explore their individual majors. This, in turn, would help them gain knowledge of the vocabulary of their individual majors and would help them gain knowledge of the pertinent issues and major authors and works in their chosen fields.

In the area of reading, it is apparent from this study that several actions need to be taken on the part of intensive English programs. First, because of the immediate need to read and digest large amounts of material from the very beginning of a semester in mainstream courses, students need to be taught how to evaluate the materials that are assigned to them and taught how to selectively read such materials, rather than just attempting to read all materials assigned to them. Additionally, intensive English program students need to be taught to read ahead in their majors. Students should be shown to use the time in between semesters as a chance to read textbooks that they will be using during the following semester, to familiarize themselves with the vocabulary contained in the textbooks, and to familiarize themselves with the issues in their individual majors. Toward this end, intensive English program instructors need to be prepared to assist their students in determining what texts will be required of them in subsequent semesters.

While virtually all of the informants in the present study had been taught how to do library research in IEP writing classes, all of them nevertheless expressed difficulty with the process. As a way to solve this problem, it is apparent that more emphasis needs to be placed on helping students learn how to find their way through the large amount of materials that they are encountering, helping them determine how to judge what materials are useful and which are not, and helping them learn how to narrow down research topics to more manageable sizes. Additionally, more emphasis needs to be placed on helping students overcome their fear of using technology so that they can more fully use these tools to sort through materials and narrow topics. The present study suggests, further, that this instruction on the research process will only be effective if it is done on a continuing basis throughout the students' time in the intensive English program.

Additional instruction is also needed on technology in general and helping students get over technology shock. Toward this end, more explicit instruction on the terminology of technology is needed, helping students put words to the actions that they have previously learned through their own trial and error.

The present study would also suggest that more explicit instruction on understanding academic culture is needed. Once again, because all informants' experiences were so different from each other, emphasis should be placed on leading students to discover the basic rhythms of their majors, as well as the activities, events, and inter-group relationships contained therein.

Such explicit instruction on the culture of the classroom should also include explicit training on how to interact with instructors, the present research would suggest. Especially important is instruction on how to speak more directly to an instructor when the student is having difficulties. In addition, the present research would suggest that students need to be taught that it is their responsibility to accommodate themselves to the teaching/learning patterns of a particular course.

Also suggested by the present research is the need for more comprehensive training and practice in participating in group work and presentations. Because of the varied forms of both group work and presentation projects encountered by the informants, this study would suggest that this training and practice needs to be included in all of the different skill areas studied in the IEP, not just in speaking, and that as many different types of group projects and presentation forms as possible need to be included.

Similarly, it is apparent from the present research that IEP students need more training and practice with different types of examination styles and text types. Once again, because of the wide variety of test and text types encountered, this study suggests that these different types of tests and texts need to be included in as many different IEP courses as possible, in as many forms as possible. Also needed is more explicit experience in and training for dealing with different types of classroom set-ups, especially experience in dealing with laboratory settings and large class sizes.

The need for more explicit instruction in asking questions of instructors in the classroom is also indicated by the present research. This instruction needs to take two forms to be fully effective. On the one hand, this study indicates that informants need specific instruction on how to formulate questions. IEPs also need to help students deal with the conflict between the need to express their ideas clearly and directly (especially in the American academic cultural context) and the fact that their home cultures often emphasize the need to be respectful towards their teachers by speaking indirectly. Toward this end, it is suggested that the IEP continue and widen its practice of taking students in listening and speaking classes to academic lectures on campus. These experiences provide students with the opportunity to be exposed to a wide variety of individual voices and accents and to analyze instructor-student interactions in American classrooms. In addition, students have the chance to practice note taking in a variety of "real world" classroom settings.

Further, the present study indicates that students need more explicit instruction regarding their entry into mainstream university programs. Students should first of all be encouraged to make a more concerted effort to establish relationships with others in their major, since these people provide the opportunity to discuss homework assignments, help students determine how and what to study for tests, and provide opportunities for clarifying questions. Students also need to be encouraged to approach their mainstream instructors at the beginning of the semester, explaining to the instructor their linguistic difficulties and demonstrating their willingness to learn. Additionally, students need to be taught how to physically position themselves in the classroom throughout the semester to gain the maximum benefit while minimizing distractions. International students should also be given more explicit information on what extra help is available to them in their academic programs. And finally, it would be particularly useful if ongoing guidance along the preceding lines could be provided during international students' first semester in their mainstream classes.

Recommendations for further research

1. This study looked at the experiences of international students' transition to mainstream university courses during one semester only. Because the experiences of these informants is ever changing and expanding, it would be informative to follow a group of informants not only during the first semester of their transition, but through their entire university experience.

2. This study also looked at the experiences of a limited number of informants, from a limited number of countries and cultural backgrounds. Therefore, a larger study which would include informants from larger numbers of countries, as well as other ethnic and language groups, would be highly beneficial as a way to discover more about the nature of the transition from an intensive English program to mainstream university courses.

3. Additionally, although this study looked at the transition process from the viewpoint of the international students themselves as they were making the transition, a second viewpoint, that of the instructors who teach these international students, needs to be addressed.

4. More follow-up is definitely needed to examine how test anxiety is being interpreted (or misinterpreted) by the instructors of international students in mainstream classes.

5. More research also needs to be conducted that examines more closely the experiences of international students as they participate in group projects and group presentations in mainstream American university classes.

6. Finally, more research needs to be undertaken that examines the experiences of international students as they attempt to master and use the American university library and the accompanying computer systems.

Bibliography

Applebee, A. N. (1981). *Writing in the secondary school: English and the content areas*. Urbana, IL: National Council of Teachers of English.

Atkinson, D., & Ramanathan, V. (1995). Cultures of writing: An ethnographic comparison of L1 and L2 university writing/language programs. *TESOL Quarterly, 29*(3), 539-568.

Barrett, R. P. (1982). Introduction. In R. P. Barrett (Ed.), *The administration of intensive English language programs* (pp. 1-5). Washington, D.C.: National Association for Foreign Student Affairs.

Bernard, H. R. (1995). *Research methods in cultural anthropology*. Newbury Park, CA: Sage Publications.

Christison, M. A., & Krahnke, K. J. (1986). Student perceptions of academic language study. *TESOL Quarterly, 20*(1), 61-79.

Clarke, M. A. (1994). "Mainstreaming" ESL students: Disturbing changes. *College ESL, 4*(1), 1-19.

Diesing, P. (1971). *Patterns of discovery in the social sciences*. Chicago: Aldine.

Duff, P. A. (2001). Language, literacy, content, and (pop) culture: Challenges for ESL students in mainstream courses. *The Canadian Modern Language Review, 58*(1), 103-132.

Eskey, D. E. (1997). The IEP as a nontraditional entity. In M. A. Christison & F. L. Stoller (Eds.), *A handbook for language program administrators* (pp. 21-30). Burlingame, CA: Alta Book Center.

Firth, R. (1961). *Elements of social organization*. Boston: Beacon.

Freiermuth, M. R. (2001). Native speakers or non-native speakers: Who has the floor? Online and face-to-face interaction in culturally mixed small groups. *Computer Assisted Language Learning, 14*(2), 169-199.

Geertz, C. (1973). *The interpretation of cultures*. New York: Random House.

Goffman, E. (1974). *Frame analysis: An essay on the organization of experience*. Cambridge, MA: Harvard University Press.

Gradman, H. L. & Hanania, E. (1991). Language learning background factors and ESL proficiency. *The Modern Language Journal, 75*(i), 39-51.

Harklau, L. (1994). ESL versus mainstream classes: Contrasting L2 learning environments. *TESOL Quarterly, 28*(2), 241-272.

Heath, S. B. (1982). Ethnography in education: Defining the essentials. In P. Gilmore & A. A. Glatthorn (Eds.), *Children in and out of school: Ethnography and education* (pp. 33-55). Washington, DC: Center for Applied Linguistics.

Horwitz, E. K., Horwitz, M. B., & Cope, J. (1986). Foreign language classroom anxiety. *The Modern Language Journal, 70*(ii), 125-132.

Institute of International Education. (2003, November 3). International student enrollment growth slows in 2002/2003, large gains from leading countries offset numerous decreases. Retreived December 2, 2003 from http://opendoors.iienetwork.org/?p=36523.

Johnson, D. M. (1983). Natural language learning by design: a classroom experiment in social interaction and second language acquisition. *TESOL Quarterly 17*(1): 55-68.

Kaplan, R. B. (1997). An IEP is a many-splendored thing. In M. A. Christison & F. L. Stoller (Eds.), *A handbook for language program administrators* (pp. 3-19). Burlingame, CA: Alta Book Center.

Kelley, E., & Sweet, D. (1991, March). Transitioning from community college ESL: An ethnographic approach. Paper presented at the Annual Meeting of the *Teachers of English to Speakers of Other Languages*, New York, NY.

Leki, I. (1999). "Pretty much I screwed up": Ill-served needs of a permanent resident. In L. Harklau, K. M. Losey, and M. Siegal (Eds.), *Generation 1.5 Meets College Composition: Issues in the Teaching of Writing to U.S.-Educated Learners of ESL* (pp. 17-43). Mahwah, N.J.: Lawrence Erlbaum Associates.

Leki, I., & Carson, J. G. (1994). Students' perceptions of EAP writing instruction and writing needs across the disciplines. *TESOL Quarterly, 28*(1), 81-101.

Lucas, T. & Wagner, S. (1999). Facilitating secondary English language learners' transition into the mainstream. *TESOL Journal, 8*(4), 6-13.

Lutz, F. W. (1981). Ethnography - The holistic approach to understanding schooling. In J. L. Green and C. Wallat (Eds.), *Ethnography and language in educational settings* (pp. 51-63). Norwood, NJ: ABLEX Publishing Corporation.

Malinowski, B. (1922). *Argonauts of the Western Pacific.* London: Routledge and Kegan Paul.

Mehan, H. (1979). *Learning lessons.* Cambridge, MA: Harvard University Press.

Miller, J. M. (2000). Language use, identity, and social interaction: Migrant students in Australia. *Research on Language and Social Interaction, 33*(1), 69-100.

Narroll, R., & Cohen, R. (1973). *A handbook of methods in cultural anthropology.* New York: Natural History Press.

Ostler, S. E. (1980). A survey of academic needs for advanced ESL. *TESOL Quarterly, 16*(4), 489-502.

Pelto, P., & Pelto, G. (1970). *Anthropological research: The structure of inquiry.* New York: Harper and Row.

Perdreau, C. (1994). Roles, responsibilities, and priorities of the intensive English program. *Journal of Intensive English Studies, 8*, 1-25.

Pica, T., & Doughty, C. (1985). Input and interaction in the communicative language classroom: A comparison to teacher-fronted and group activities. In S. M. Gass and C. G. Madden (Eds.), *Input in second language acquisition* (pp. 115-132). Rowley, MA: Newbury House,.

Pike, K. L. (1964). *Language in relation to a unified theory of structures of human behavior.* The Hague: Mouton.

Rubin, J. (1975). What the "good language learner" can teach us. *TESOL Quarterly, 9*(1), 41-51.

Saville-Troike, M. (1984). What *really* matters in second language learning for academic achievement? *TESOL Quarterly, 18*(2), 199-219.

Selinker, L., Todd Trimble, R. M., & Trimble, L. (1976). Presuppositional rhetorical information in EST discourse. *TESOL Quarterly, 10*(3), 281-290.

Sevigny, M. J. (1981). Triangulated inquiry - A methodology for the analysis of classroom interaction. In J. Green and C. Wallat (Eds.), *Ethnography and language in educational settings* (pp. 65-81). Norwood, NJ: ABLEX Publishing Corporation.

Shannon, S. M. (1990). Transition from bilingual programs to all-English programs: Issues about and beyond language. *Linguistics and Education, 2*, 323-343.

Shuck, G. (1995). Preparing for university writing courses: A survey of students' perceptions. *Journal of Intensive English Studies, 9*, 38-49.

Skilton, E., & Meyer, T. (1993). "So what are you talking about?": The importance of student questions in the ESL classroom. *Working Papers in Educational Linguistics, 9*(2), 81-99.

Smoke, T. (1988). Using feedback from ESL students to enhance their success in college. In S. Benesch (ed.), *Ending remediation: Linking ESL and content in higher education* (pp. 7-19). Alexandria, VA: Teachers of English to Speakers of Other Languages.

Spradley, J. (1979). *The ethnographic interview.* Forth Worth, TX: Harcourt Brace Jovanovich.

Spradley, J. (1980). *Participant observation.* New York: Holt, Rinehart and Winston.

Stern, H. H. (1975). What can we learn from the good language learner? *Canadian Modern Language Review, 31,* 304-318.

Strong, M. (1983). Social styles and the second language acquisition of Spanish-speaking kindergartners. *TESOL Quarterly 17*(2), 241-258.

Watson-Gegeo, K. A. (1988). Ethnography in ESL: Defining the essentials. *TESOL Quarterly, 22*(4), 575-592.

Werner, O., & Schoepfle, G. M. (1987). *Systematic fieldwork,* (Vol. 1). Newbury Park, CA: Sage Publications.

Wilhelm, K. H. (1995, March). Identification of LL (language learning) background variables associated with university IEP success. Paper presented at the *Annual Conference of the American Association of Applied Linguistics,* Long Beach, CA.

Willett, J. (1995). Becoming first graders in an L2: An ethnographic study of L2 socialization. *TESOL Quarterly, 29*(3), 473-503.

Young, J. R. (2003, June 27). Enrollment drops in English programs. *Chronicle of Higher Education,* p. 36.

Zaharlick, A., & Green, J. (1991). Ethnographic research. In J. Flood, J.M. Jensen, D. Lapp, and J.R. Squire (Eds.), *Handbook of research on teaching the English language arts* (pp. 205-225). New York: Macmillan.

INDEX

Africa, 37, 50
American Culture, 20, 28, 53, 72, 118, 176, 212
Applebee, A.N., 16
Asia, 37, 70, 142
Atkinson, D., 195
Australia, 18
Ayla, 158
Barrett, 4
Bernard, H. R., 37, 47, 48
Bill, 19
British English, 51, 159
Canada, 19, 23
Carson (a pseudonym), 15
Carson, J. G., 179, 182
Center for English as a Second Language, 27
Christison, M. A., 23, 189
Clarke, M. A., 175
Class Observations, 43
CNN, 90
Cohen, R., 34
College/University Level, 21
Cope, J., 180
Culture Shock, 54, 72, 95, 145, 158, 160, 167, 208
Developmental English, 26
Diesing, P., 34
Discovery Channel, 95, 113
Doughty, C., 188
Duff, P. A., 19
Elementary School Level, 11
emic vs. *etic*, 33
English Language Institute, 4
Eskey, D., 4, 6
Ethnography, 3, 31
Example Questions, 39

Experience Questions, 39
Fernanda, 116
Firth, R., 34
French, 50, 158
Freiermuth, M. R., 191
Geertz, C., 32
German, 158
Goffman, E., 191
Goodman, A. 2, 4
Gradman, H. L., 175, 185
Grand Tour Questions, 39
Green, J., 32, 35
Hanania, E., 175, 185
Harklau, L., 11, 14, 176, 177, 184, 194, 197, 203, 204, 222
Heath, S. B., 32
Horwitz, E. K., 180
Horwitz, M. B., 180
Hunter College, 24
Institute of International Education, 1, 2, 4
Interviews, 38
Jan, 28
Johnson, D. M., 185
Journal, 47
Kaplan, R., 4
Kelley, E., 25, 193
Krahnke, K. J., 23, 189
Learning Center, 105, 114, 150, 187, 197, 215
Leki, I., 28, 179, 182
Lucas, T., 184
Lutz, F. W., 32
Lyn, 142
Malinowski, B., 32
Massachusetts, 25
Mari, 70

Mehan, H., 185
Middle East, 37, 158
Miller, J. M., 18
Mini Tour Questions, 39
Meyer, T., 188
Narroll, R., 34
Open Doors 2002, 1, 2
Ostler, S. E., 21, 181, 184, 190, 191, 193, 194, 201, 205, 206
Pam, 19
Peace Corps, 52
Pelto, P., 34
Pelto, G., 34
Perdreau, C., 205
Pica, T., 188
Pike, K. L., 33
Poland, 28
Ramanathan, V., 195
Records, 46
Rubin, J., 201
Romulo, 91
Puerto Rico, 26
Samory, 50
Saville-Troike, M., 173
San Francisco, 14
Schoepfle, G. M., 32, 33, 36, 38, 46, 47
Secondary School Level, 14
Selinker, L., 194
Sevigny, M. J., 31

Shannon, S. M., 11
Shuck, G., 27, 181, 186, 202, 205
Skilton, E., 188
Smoke, T., 2, 24, 180, 192, 193, 198, 201
South America, 37, 91, 116
Speech Pathology, 55, 119, 198, 218
Spradley, J., 32, 33, 36, 38, 39, 46, 47, 48
Stern, H. H., 176, 182, 187
Strong, M., 185
Sweet, D., 25, 193
Transcripts, 48
Todd Trimble, R. M., 194
TOEFL, 41, 63, 65, 159
Trimble, L., 194
UNICEF, 53
The University, 36, 37, 213
University of Arizona, 27
University of Southern California, 21
Wagner, S., 184
Watson-Gegeo, K. A., 31, 32, 33, 34, 35, 36
Werner, O., 32, 33, 36, 38, 46, 47
Wilhelm, K. H., 175
Willetts, J., 13
Young, 2
Zaharlick, A., 32, 35

MELLEN STUDIES IN EDUCATION

1. C. J. Schott, **Improving The Training and Evaluation of Teachers at the Secondary School Level: Educating the Educators in Pursuit of Excellence**
2. Manfred Prokop, **Learning Strategies For Second Language Users: An Analytical Appraisal with Case Studies**
3. Charles P. Nemeth, **A Status Report on Contemporary Criminal Justice Education: A Definition of the Discipline and an Assessment of Its Curricula, Faculty and Program Characteristics**
4. Stephen H. Barnes (ed.), **Points of View on American Higher Education: A Selection of Essays from** *The Chronicle of Higher Education* **(Volume 1) Professors and Scholarship**
5. Stephen H. Barnes (ed.), **Points of View on American Higher Education: A Selection of Essays from** *The Chronicle of Higher Education* **(Volume 2) Institutions and Issues**
6. Stephen H. Barnes (ed.), **Points of View on American Higher Education: A Selection of Essays from** *The Chronicle of Higher Education* **(Volume 3) Students and Standards**
7. Michael V. Belok and Thomas Metos, **The University President in Arizona 1945-1980: An Oral History**
8. Henry R. Weinstock and Charles J. Fazzaro, **Democratic Ideals and the Valuing of Knowledge In American Education: Two Contradictory Tendencies**
9. Arthur R. Crowell, Jr., **A Handbook For the Special Education Administrator: Organization and Procedures for Special Education**
10. J.J. Chambliss, **The Influence of Plato and Aristotle on John Dewey's Philosophy**
11. Alan H. Levy, **Elite Education and the Private School: Excellence and Arrogance at Phillips Exeter Academy**
12. James J. Van Patten (ed.), **Problems and Issues in College Teaching and Higher Education Leadership**
13. Célestin Freinet, **The Wisdom of Matthew: An Essay in Contemporary French Educational Theory**, John Sivell (trans.)
14. Francis R. Phillips, **Bishop Beck and English Education, 1949-1959**
15. Gerhard Falk, **The Life of the Academic Professional in America: An Inventory of Tasks, Tensions & Achievements**
16. Phillip Santa Maria, **The Question of Elementary Education in the Third Russian State Duma, 1907-1912**
17. James J. Van Patten (ed.), **The Socio-Cultural Foundations of Education and the Evolution of Education Policies in the U.S.**
18. Peter P. DeBoer, **Origins of Teacher Education at Calvin Colege, 1900-1930: And Gladly Teach**
19. Célestin Freinet, **Education Through Work: A Model for Child-Centered Learning**, John Sivell (trans.)
20. John Sivell (ed.), **Freinet Pedagogy: Theory and Practice**
21. John Klapper, **Foreign-Language Learning Through Immersion**
22. Maurice Whitehead, **The Academies of the Reverend Bartholomew Booth in Georgian England and Revolutionary America**
23. Margaret D. Tannenbaum, **Concepts and Issues in School Choice**
24. Rose M. Duhon-Sells and Emma T. Pitts, **An Interdisciplinary Approach to Multicultural Teaching and Learning**
25. Robert E. Ward, **An Encyclopedia of Irish Schools, 1500-1800**

26. David A. Brodie, **A Reference Manual for Human Performance Measurement in the Field of Physical Education and Sports Sciences**
27. Xiufeng Liu, **Mathematics and Science Curriculum Change in the People's Republic of China**
28. Judith Evans Longacre, **The History of Wilson College 1868 to 1970**
29. Thomas E. Jordan, **The First Decade of Life, Volume I: Birth to Age Five**
30. Thomas E. Jordan, **The First Decade of Life, Volume II: The Child From Five to Ten Years**
31. Mary I. Fuller and Anthony J. Rosie (eds.), **Teacher Education and School Partnerships**
32. James J. Van Patten (ed.), **Watersheds in Higher Education**
33. K. (Moti) Gokulsing and Cornel DaCosta (eds.), **Usable Knowledges as the Goal of University Education: Innovations in the Academic Enterprise Culture**
34. Georges Duquette (ed.), **Classroom Methods and Strategies for Teaching at the Secondary Level**
35. Linda A. Jackson and Michael Murray, **What Students Really Think of Professors: An Analysis of Classroom Evaluation Forms at an American University**
36. Donald H. Parkerson and Jo Ann Parkerson, **The Emergence of the Common School in the U.S. Countryside**
37. Neil R. Fenske, **A History of American Public High Schools, 1890-1990: Through the Eyes of Principals**
38. Gwendolyn M. Duhon Boudreaux (ed.), **An Interdisciplinary Approach to Issues and Practices in Teacher Education**
39. John Roach, **A Regional Study of Yorkshire Schools 1500-1820**
40. V.J. Thacker, **Using Co-operative Inquiry to Raise Awareness of the Leadership and Organizational Culture in an English Primary School**
41. Elizabeth Monk-Turner, **Community College Education and Its Impact on Socioeconomic Status Attainment**
42. George A. Churukian and Corey R. Lock (eds.), **International Narratives on Becoming a Teacher Educator: Pathways to a Profession**
43. Cecilia G. Manrique and Gabriel G. Manrique, **The Multicultural or Immigrant Faculty in American Society**
44. James J. Van Patten (ed.), **Challenges and Opportunities for Education in the 21st Century**
45. Barry W. Birnbaum, **Connecting Special Education and Technology for the 21st Century**
46. J. David Knottnerus and Frédérique Van de Poel-Knottnerus, **The Social Worlds of Male and Female Children in the Nineteenth Century French Educational System: Youth, Rituals, and Elites**
47. Sandra Frey Stegman, **Student Teaching in the Choral Classroom: An Investigation of Secondary Choral Music Student Teachers' Perceptions of Instructional Successes and Problems as They Reflect on Their Music Teaching**
48. Gwendolyn M. Duhon and Tony Manson (eds.), **Preparation, Collaboration, and Emphasis on the Family in School Counseling for the New Millennium**
49. Katherina Danko-McGhee, **The Aesthetic Preferences of Young Children**
50. Jane Davis-Seaver, **Critical Thinking in Young Children**
51. Gwendolyn M. Duhon and Tony J. Manson (eds.), **Implications for Teacher Education – Cross-Ethnic and Cross-Racial Dynamics of Instruction**

52. Samuel Mitchell, **Partnerships in Creative Activities Among Schools, Artists and Professional Organizations Promoting Arts Education**
53. Loretta Niebur, **Incorporating Assessment and the National Standards for Music Education into Everyday Teaching**
54. Tony Del Valle, **Written Literacy Features of Three Puerto Rican Family Networks in Chicago: An Ethnographic Study**
55. Christine J. Villani and Colin C. Ward, **Violence and Non-Violence in the Schools: A Manual for Administration**
56. Michael Dallaire, **Contemplation in Liberation – A Method for Spiritual Education in the Schools**
57. Gwendolyn M. Duhon, **Problems and Solutions in Urban Schools**
58. Paul Grosch, **Recognition of the Spirit and Its Development as Legitimate Concerns of Education**
59. D. Antonio Cantu, **An Investigation of the Relationship Between Social Studies Teachers' Beliefs and Practice**
60. Loretta Walton Jaggers, Nanthalia W. McJamerson and Gwendolyn M. Duhon (eds.), **Developing Literacy Skills Across the Curriculum: Practical, Approaches, Creative Models, Strategies, and Resources**
61. Haim Gordon and Rivca Gordon, **Sartre's Philosophy and the Challenge of Education**
62. Robert D. Buchanan and Ruth Ann Roberts, **Performance-Based Evaluation for Certificated and Non-Certificated School Personnel: Standards, Criteria, Indicators, Models**
63. C. David Warner III, **Opinions of Administrators, Faculty, and Students Regarding Academic Freedom and Student Artistic Expression**
64. Robert D. Heslep, **A Philosophical Guide for Decision Making by Educators: Developing a Set of Foundational Principles**
65. Noel P. Hurley, **How You Speak Determines How You Learn: Resource Allocation and Student Achievement**
66. Barry W. Birnbaum, **Foundations and Practices in the Use of Distance Education**
67. Franklin H. Silverman and Robert Moulton, **The Impact of a Unique Cooperative American University USAID Funded Speech-Language Pathologist, Audiologist, and Deaf Educator B.S. Degree Program in the Gaza Strip**
68. Tony J. Manson (ed.), **Teacher Education Preparation for Diversity**
69. Scott D. Robinson, **Autobiostories Promoting Emotional Insights into the Teaching and Learning of Secondary Science**
70. Francis Oakley, **The Leadership Challenge of a College Presidency: Meaning, Occasion, and Voice**
71. Melvin D. Williams, **The Ethnography of an Anthropology Department, 1959-1979: An Academic Village**
72. Kevin McGuinness, **The Concept of Academic Freedom**
73. Alastair Sharp, **Reading Comprehension and Text Organization**
74. Nicholas Beattie, **The Freinet Movements of France, Italy, and Germany, 1920-2000: Versions of Educational Progressivism**
75. Anne P. Chapman, **Language Practices in School Mathematics: A Social Semiotic Approach**
76. Wendy Robinson, **Pupil Teachers and Their Professional Training in Pupil-Teacher Centres in England and Wales, 1870-1914**
77. Barbara A. Sposet, **The Affective and Cognitive Development of Culture Learning During the Early and Middle Childhood Curriculum**

78. John P. Anchan and Shiva S. Halli, **Exploring the Role of the Internet in Global Education**
79. James J. Van Patten and Timothy J. Bergen, **A Case Study Approach to a Multi-Cultural Mosaic in Education**
80. Jeffrey L. Hoogeveen, **The Role of Students in the History of Composition**
81. Rose M. Duhon-Sells and Leslie Agard-Jones (eds.), **Educators Leading the Challenge to Alleviate School Violence**
82. Rose Marie Duhon-Sells, Halloway C. Sells, Alice Duhon-Ross, Gwendolyn Duhon, Glendolyn Duhon-JeanLouis (eds.) **International Perspectives on Methods of Improving Education Focusing on the Quality of Diversity**
83. Ruth Rees, **A New Era in Educational Leadership–One Principal, Two Schools: Twinning**
84. Daniel J. Mahoney, **An Organizational, Social-Psychological, and Ethical Analysis of School Administrators' Use of Deception**
85. Judith Longacre, **The Trial and Renewal of Wilson College**
86. Michael Delucchi, **Student Satisfaction with Higher Education During the 1970s—A Decade of Social Change**
87. Samuel Mitchell, **The Value of Educational Partnerships Worldwide with the Arts, Science, Business, and Community Organizations**
88. Susan Davis Lenski and Wendy L. Black (eds.), **Transforming Teacher Education Through Partnerships**
89. Ana Maria Klein, **Learning How Children Process Mathematical Problems**
90. Laura Shea Doolan, **The History of the International Learning Styles Network and Its Impact on Educational Innovation**
91. Gail Singleton Taylor (ed.), **The Impact of High-Stakes Testing on the Academic Futures of Non-Mainstream Students**
92. G.R. Evans, **Inside the University of Cambridge in the Modern World**
93. Agnes D. Walkinshaw, **Integrating Drama with Primary and Junior Education: The Ongoing Debate**
94. Joe Marshall Hardin and Ray Wallace (eds.), **Teaching, Research, and Service in the Twenty-First Century English Department: A Delicate Balance**
95. Samuel Mitchell, Patricia Klinck and John Burger (eds.), **Worldwide Partnerships for Schools with Voluntary Organizations, Foundations, Universities, Companies and Community Councils**
96. Emerson D. Case, **Making the Transition from an Intensive English Program to Mainstream University Courses–An Ethnographic Study**